This book is dedicated to a lot of people (noted in the **Acknowledgements**), but mainly, to my father Stu.

He taught me to be a "normal" pop culture fanatic.
He taught me how to save money for fun & security.
He taught me how to get good travel deals.
He always encourages what I do, even if he doesn't understand what I'm doing at the time.

But I just can't get into Barry Manilow's music like he is. Sorry, dad. "Everything's gonna be alright." - *Amanda*

Fan Guide to "Destination Truth"

Written, Curated & Edited by:
Amanda Rosenblatt

Cryptid, Ghost & Case Descriptions by:
Brad Acevedo

Additional Quotes from:
Joshua Gates, Other *DT* Cast Members & Fellow Fans

Cover Art & Back of Book designed by:
Amanda Rosenblatt through *Canva.com* software

Various Graphics in this Book
are Free Use from *Pixabay.com*

TABLE OF CONTENTS

- Foreword by Joshua Gates
- Preface from the Author
- Chapter 1 - Season One
- Chapter 2 - The Host
- Chapter 3 - Season Two
- Chapter 4 - DT Crew
- Chapter 5 - Season Three
- Chapter 6 - Fan Q's & Evidence
- Chapter 7 - Season Four
- Chapter 8 - DT Fans
- Chapter 9 - Season Five
- Acknowledgements

FOREWORD BY JOSHUA GATES
Dated May 2nd, 2016
Sent from somewhere in Nepal around 3 a.m. Pacific Time

I can hardly believe that it's been almost 4 years since we aired the final episode of *Destination Truth*. A lot has changed for me since then, though, as I sit here scribbling away in a frigid tea-house in the Himalayas, perhaps not as much as I think. On one hand, I now helm an all-new series for Travel Channel called *Expedition Unknown*, I'm married, and I'm a father. On the other hand, I'm still living out of a suitcase and exploring the world's most enduring legends while driving a lot of crappy vehicles.

When I look back at the episodes of *Destination Truth* recounted in the pages that follow, waves of memories and emotions come washing over me. More than anything, I find myself marveling at how many unlikely adventures we managed to pull off. We conducted the first-ever overnight filming in King Tut's tomb, the first ever overnight shoot at the Temple of Angkor Wat, and the world's most far-flung paranormal investigation in Antarctica. We explored the remote forests of Siberia, the mountains of Nepal, and the snake-infested rain forests of the Amazon. Hell, we even spent a radioactive night in the ruins of Chernobyl. I'm so proud and forever indebted to my crew who followed me to the ends of the Earth (literally), and risked life and limb to chronicle these and other investigations.

The show was both hilariously fun, and, at times, enormously difficult to film. Some days were a laugh-a-minute. I'll never forget Evan dressing up like a local or trying to juggle watermelons in Egypt. I'll never forget goofing around in markets with Gabe and Mike, watching Jael try to ride a horse, or laughing my ass off with Ryder as we tried to reenact the pottery scene from *Ghost*.

Other days weren't so enjoyable. Memories of getting violently ill in Micronesia, dangling over a mine shaft in Chile, or having the roof rip off my plane in Romania are perhaps best left in the rear view mirror. But, most days felt like an absolute privilege and will stay with me forever.

Perhaps my strongest memory of the series is of the fans. The fact is, *Destination Truth* was a show that burned bright because of our incredible viewership. From the very beginning, *DT* garnered the grassroots support of passionate fans who embraced our merry band of explorers and kept tuning in week after week to see what kind of trouble we'd get them into next. For her part, the author of this book has been one of our most stalwart supporters, and I'm deeply appreciative of Amanda's efforts to not only promote the show, but to bring together our most loyal viewers.

I want to thank each and every one of you who tuned in. You were right there with us along the bumpy roads, in the darkest jungles, and in the craziest situations. Thanks for being a part of Team Truth.

I hope you enjoyed the adventure as much as I did,
and I can't wait to see you all out on the road.

Cheers,
Josh Gates

PREFACE FROM THE AUTHOR

Hi, fellow fans. I'll just say first and foremost to rest your fears that I promise this book is not all about me. It's about ALL of us, the cast and crew of the show, and what this show means to us. I have many stories from you and from the cast in here, but considering all the years I've been mistaken for Josh online when I've spent hours upon hours editing websites and videos, updating social media pages, traveling to conventions, taking overnight flights or buses from events when I still had to report to work the next morning, and waiting in long lines at the post office, I figure I've earned a couple of pages here. God, I hope that doesn't make me sound entitled.

When I was in college, I took the saying of applying our classes to real world experiences to heart. I've always been a fan of learning, plus when you're paying so much for a college education in America, you might as well get some real-world use out of it.

When it came to my computer science course, numbers and I did not get along - dealing with coding was a struggle, and the struggle was real. The teacher, though, was very fair and patient. His humor reminded me a lot of Josh Gates, which I guess is appropriate, considering my journey. I was struck with a random idea one night before falling asleep in my dorm room that ended up changing my life.

It was 2008 and social media was starting to heat up - Myspace was on a bit of a death rattle, Facebook was still chugging along, YouTube was a fairly new sensation, and Twitter was about to burst in popularity. I considered how big of a fan I was of Josh, as well as the series *Destination Truth* and as I recall, we got extra credit for starting our own website for that computer science course. Either way, ironically, I don't even think I ended up showing my fan page to that professor.

I did rigorous research beforehand so I wouldn't be stepping on the toes of other fans, nor did I want to accidentally commit plagiarism. Besides an inactive Myspace *Destination Truth* fan-made page, I saw I was good to go. Though the site and corresponding Twitter plus Facebook accounts were originally under a different name, *Singularity Fan Pages* was born.

Starting this hobby site and learning my way around emerging social media taught me many skills. I got to meet lots of amazing people both online and offline, including some people who didn't like me or what I did so much, so that was a new experience in how big the internet could be.

I recall being invited to the Syfy brand relaunch of July 2009 in New York City, which was the first time I traveled anywhere by myself that wasn't related to college. It was cool to be considered Press for the first time since graduating with a Journalism degree, but was admittedly having a hard time finding a job in my field.

At this event, I met Josh for the first time. It was cool to be face to face with someone I loved watching on TV and did so many cool things with their life. He said he looked forward to reaching out to more fans with me, and years later, it's crazy to think how far on this journey we both have come.

Josh has published a book, has been on popular TV shows, won awards, has gotten married, has visited 100 countries, and has an adorable little baby boy named Owen. Myself?

I've traveled all across the country under the kindness of strangers. I've crossed items off my bucket list, like attending San Diego Comic Con and traveling internationally. I met my significant other at one of the Josh fan meet-ups that I coordinated (he also helped me write parts of this book on cryptids and ghosts). The last time I held my beloved childhood dog in my arms before her passing, the same dog that would bark in the background during many a *DT Fan Radio* episode, was while watching a *DT* marathon on TV and being able to laugh at the antics on the show, despite my sadness of the state she was in. On a happier note, I've even held a few paid content and social media jobs in my field of study because of all this! I also learned to avoid Balut eggs at all costs.

One of the most significant moments in doing this fan work, other than people at conventions randomly recognizing me and thanking me for the time I've put in, involves one fellow fan, in particular. Kellie was from Louisiana and was an older woman with some significant health problems, but was one of the nicest people you could ever hope to meet online.

Kellie wanted to be the first fan on an episode of *Destination Truth*, but other than fans never being involved in the show's filming, her end-stage congestive heart failure would have prevented her from achieving this goal. She ended up becoming friends with myself and a tight-nit band of fellow *DT* fans, which meant a lot to her, but I wanted to do more.

I was able to coordinate the cast members to send her autographs and speak with her on my fan radio show, at the time called *DT Fan Radio*. She asked a question of Josh, Erin Ryder & Brad Kuhlman, and after they answered, she interjected wanting to say how good of a person I was and thanked me. It choked me up and it was humbling. I even felt bad she took her valuable time to speak to the cast to say that, as weird as it seems.

 **Josh Gates** ⊘
@joshuagates

 Following

Just learned that DT fan @heavenlygirl40 has passed away. Sincere condolences to her family and friends. My thoughts are with you.

RETWEETS LIKES
38   26

3:03 AM - 27 Oct 2012

Kellie passed away in October 2012 and fans like her, my friends, my family, my significant other Brad, past *DT* crew members, & Josh, shaped and shared this journey with me. That being said, I leave you with this:

Don't let anyone ever tell you that being a fan of something will get you nowhere in life, or that it means nothing. You take from it what you need and sometimes, find more than you were looking for.

My name is Amanda Rosenblatt, your fan site runner and the author of this book, and I truly hope you enjoy this fan chronology of *Destination Truth*!

CHAPTER I:
INTRO TO *DT* & SEASON ONE

Destination Truth as we know it was not always what we saw on TV. The concept was created by Neil Mandt and there was a pilot with a host other than Josh Gates. The folks over at Syfy (then known as SciFi) and NBC were not feeling it.

Luckily, our host-with-the-most was a lover of travel and just happened to be on the road chasing some of his bucket list items down with friends, so Neil was able to recommend Josh as the best and most authentic replacement. This again attests to the overall message from the Preface of this book that following your passions can pay off.

DT was a companion to *Ghost Hunters* and ended up being just as much a fan favorite as the anchor program. The show changed hands with production companies and each season, the vibe of the show changed.

The program touched on paranormal hauntings, much like *Ghost Hunters*, but it also heavily featured travel, including infamously bad rental cars, and crypto-zoologic components. *DT* was even given similar airtime opportunities, such as a live special that took place in Season 4 and a small run of merchandising.

This book contains cast interviews, a small section dedicated to the fans, and it has brief episode guides for each season (no outcomes or spoilers, since I want to make sure this book follows proper Fair Use Copyright standards), plus fun Easter Eggs like funny quotes and answers to popular fan questions about certain episodes.

I also highly recommend you get Josh's book *Memoirs of a Monster Hunter* and purchase *DT* episodes on iTunes & Amazon. Season 1 is the only one ever put physically on DVD.

Season 1, Episode 1
Destination: Papua New Guinea
Cases: The Iguanadon & The Ri Mermaid
Original Air Date: June 6th, 2007

"Living Dinosaur" is a niche in Cryptozoological study that pertains to the belief that there just might be some of those famed Thunder Lizards still inhabiting modern day Earth. We're not talking about Tyrannosaurs cloned and put on display for tourists, only to escape and munch on toilet-bound lawyers.

The Iguanodon averaged about 40 feet in length, was a member of the Hadrosaur classification of dinosaurs, and was famed for it's distinctive thumb spike. This development of recent sightings presents a much-too-intriguing and enigmatic mystery for our esteemed *DT* team to pass up.

In terms of the second case, Mermaid stories have dated as far back as 1000 B.C. These creatures have since permeated virtually every aspect of popular culture, from lovable cartoon depictions to stories of the Sirens - alluring enchantresses that would pull seafarers to their doom.

The *DT* team investigates sightings of the aquatic enigmas during their extended stay in the Guinean islands, with the investigation taking them below the waves on the hunt for elusive Oceania region mysteries.

Josh: "You would not believe the Captain that we had on this flight. This guy comes on & he says 'Ladies & Gentlemen - Welcome to London.' There was this long beat & he was like, 'Excuse me, Auckland.' No kidding - he had no idea where he had flown to!"

Josh: "Spring Break: Papua New Guinea! Where is Marc Carter & does he have his pants on?"

Josh: "Excuse me! The gentleman with the M16?"

Season 1, Episode 2
Destinations: Thailand -
Khon Kean & the Mekong River
Cases: Haunted Village & The Naga
Original Air Date: June 13th, 2007

Thailand is a country rich in culture and folklore, which is a statement that can only inevitably lead to tales of the supernatural. The Thai boast mystical stories ranging from one-legged vampires to disembodied floating heads. With such a diverse lore in tradition and mythology, who knows what Josh and the team might encounter?

 Their journey takes them to the Khon Kaen province in search of a village that many claim to be haunted by ghosts of the past. Afterwards, we travel the waters of the Mekong to investigate alleged sightings of The Naga.

A type of deity represented in many South Eastern Asian religions as massive, serpentine spirits, the Naga traditionally seem to straddle the line of good and evil. Author Rudyard Kipling even went so far as to name the villains in his story *Rikki Tiki Tavi* after these snake-like aggressors.

Along the banks of the Mekong river, will the identity of these mystical beings be revealed by our intrepid crew?

FUNNY QUOTES THIS EPISODE

Josh VO (Voiceover): "I wanted to stick around & see if these two had a method for hunting Bigfoot. I'm sure it would involve a banana & a lasso, but it was getting late."

Josh: "How will he stop the boat from moving?" **Boat Crew Member:** "STOP the boat from moving?" **Josh:** "(pauses in silence) I don't think this guy's got an anchor."

Josh VO: "After packing our gear, I headed back to town to track down our trusty guide, who in *Scooby-Doo* fashion, had decided to flee the scene in the middle of the night."

Season 1, Episode 3
Destinations: Papua New Guinea & Chile
Cases: The Ropen & the Chupacabra
Original Air Date: June 20th, 2007

Once again, Josh and the crew delve into the alluring lore of Living Dinosaurs. This particular investigation leads back to Papua New Guinea in search of a local terror of the skies called The Ropen.

Pterosaurs are not classified as true dinosaurs, rather representing their own class of flying reptiles. What makes the Ropen (an alleged pterosaur) a particularly interesting legend are their propensity for grave robbing and alleged bio-luminesence.

One geeky pop culture coincidence cannot be discounted: The team pays a visit to a Margaritaville cabana during their investigation, but Josh turned them away back on their mission in the hot jungle instead of downing icy, adult beverages. Eight years later, Steven Spielberg and Colin Trevorrow would unleash their own army of ravenous pterosaurs upon another Margaritaville in *Jurassic World*. The only conclusion we can draw is that the movie was made by hardcore *DT* fans because, why not?

Then, the Chupacabra is our next interesting case. Making its debut on the scene as recently as the 1990's, our friend El Chupacabra (translation: "goat sucker") bears an odd mishmash of traits associated to the Grays of UFO lore, the Jersey Devil of American legend, and the Krites of endearingly cheesy B-movie horror mythos.

In Latin American regions, these creatures are distinctive for leaving behind carnage in their wake, such as dead livestock and poultry held accountable from Chupacabra attacks. They are perhaps the most prolific cryptid in modern day sightings, despite often being explained away as indigenous predators affected with mange or other physically debilitating and appearance-altering diseases.

Josh VO: "Some even suggest that the creature is a vampiric alien, or even worse - a disgruntled ex-cast member of *The Muppets*."

Josh VO: "After a minute of struggling to get this thing out of the cage, I thought he was going to pull out a bloody stump. Instead, he pulls out a ferret. Granted, the meanest damn ferret I've ever seen."

Josh: "Adenine? Thymine? Thiamine? Cytosine? What's the G one?" **Scientist:** "Guanine." **Josh**: "Three out of four is not bad! I read *Jurassic Park*. All of my knowledge of genetics comes from reading it in the ninth grade...it's just boiled down into making dinosaurs. Do you make dinosaurs here?" **Scientist**: "No." **Josh**: "That's a shame."

Season 1, Episode 4
Destinations: Malaysia & Argentina
Cases: Bigfoot & Nahuelito
Original Air Date: June 27th, 2007

Bigfoot. No nickname conjures more thoughts about the hunt for mysterious animals. Rising into prominence in the mid-1900s, Bigfoot (or the Sasquatch and the Yeti, etc.) is the hairy poster-child for all things cryptid. Whether he's tossing around Alice Cooper or palling around with John Lithgow, the creature has become a bit of a pop culture giant.

Yet despite all the commercialism and kitschiness surrounding the beast, there are those who would rather take a more scientific view of the massive biped. Sightings spread from the North-Western USA to various parts of the world. It is this alleged world-spanning distribution that leads the *DT* team into the heart of Malaysia's Endau-Rompin National Park.

Much like the large hairy hominids, there exists an equally popular cryptid: the lake monster. Indisputably, the Loch Ness Monster AKA Nessie is the most famous of these beasties, but one lake in South America plays host to its own version of the tale. The Nahuelito actually predates reports of Nessie, and is said to inhabit the Nahuel-Huapi lake in Northern Argentina.

Explanations range from the usual suspects (misidentified animals) to the prehistoric (vestigial plesiosaurs) to the 1950's sci-fi (allegations of a nuclear waste fueled mutation). Photos and video evidence of the creature exist, but Gates and team would prefer a more hands-on experience, as they make their effort to locate the elusive animal.

Josh VO: "Presented with this description of a naked, bashful, English-speaking Bigfoot, I did what any investigator would do." **Josh**: "Okay, let's go!"

Josh: "Dude, the monkeys did a number our car! All the other cars are fine. Our car? Monkey Poo Town."

EASTER EGG: Josh's Necklace

ON SEPTEMBER 3RD 2009, A FEW YEARS BEFORE JOSH'S "MEMOIRS OF A MONSTER HUNTER" WAS PUBLISHED, JOSH WAS ASKED ON DT FAN RADIO ABOUT HIS ICONIC NECKLACE THAT HE WEARS ALL THE TIME:

Josh tells us: The necklace gets a lot of questions and it has not really been addressed. This may be the first time the necklace has ever really been addressed. The necklace is magical. No, it's not magical. It's a necklace I've had since I was a kid, and I wish there was a better story about it.

My mom's British, and when I was a kid, we used to go to England like once a year. I sort of remember getting it. It looked a little different then - it was on a different kind of chain then, and I was really young…It's such a bad story because I can't really remember where I got it, which means nothing to the mystique of the necklace. But I bought it, I had it as a kid, I always kept it, and I didn't wear it a lot as a kid. I had it in a drawer. It was in my car once I got my driver's license.

Then the clasp, the chain I had it on broke, and I think that was part of why I didn't wear it…we put it on this hemp-y kind of string, it looked kinda cool, and I started wearing it again. I started wearing it again only when I traveled. I would wear it every time I took a trip, then I would come home and I'd take it off…I don't wear it until the day we leave to go do the show, then I put it on and I keep it on until the day we get home…that's the only real story to it. It's not a microphone, but it is magical. Make sure you spread that rumor around.

SOME REFERENCES TO JOSH'S NECKLACE ON DT:

JOSH: MY NECKLACE GIVES ME ALL MY POWER - DO NOT TOUCH MY NECKLACE!" -S4, E7

RYDER: "HEY JOSH - IF YOU GET STUCK IN THERE, CAN I HAVE THE NECKLACE? I MEAN, ONLY IF YOU CAN'T GET OUT!" - S4, E9 AKA THE DT LIVE SPECIAL

Our next entry into the pantheon of deep-dwelling denizens is the Mamlambo. With a name that translates to "Brain Sucker" and an affinity for turbulent weather, this water beastie holds a fearsome reputation. Josh and company brave the literal storm on the banks of the Mzintlava River in South Africa in an effort to document this creature.

Afterwards, a Zulu inspired critter called the Tokoloshe inspires fear and trepidation amongst the citizens of Lesotho. Children and adults alike fear its name and the antagonistic sprite holds roots in local mysticism.

It is said the Tokoloshe is fond of sour milk, of all things. With a dairy distraction in tow, the team stakes out an abandoned hut in hopes of catching the phantom prankster on film.

Neil: "I accept full responsibility. This is all my fault. If we run out [of gas], I will walk through the game reserve with live animals-" **Josh**: "That is such a lie!"

Josh VO: "The sanguma explained that not only are there many people in this region scared of the Tokoloshe and actively avoid encounters with it - they also refuse to discuss its very existence, fearing retribution. It's kind of like talking about the Yankees in Boston."

Josh VO: "One eyewitness came at a price. What did this woman want for such valuable information? Money? Camera gear? One night alone with a strapping young American truth-seeker?" **Translator**: "She wants sweets." **Josh**: "Sweets!" **Josh VO**: "Nah, she just wanted candy."

Werewolf lore has existed for centuries, dating back to the myth of King Lycaeon and beyond. In Argentina, they fear a particular breed known as El Lobizon, and this belief in the beast stretches as far as the Argentinean government. Folkloric basis extends to a genealogical sense, as the 7th son in an all-male family is believed to be afflicted by these lunar transformations.

With the assistance of an actual 7th son, along with fan-favorite Carlos the dramatic wolf man mime, Josh sets off to solve the mystery. Will 7's prove to be wild in this lupine deck, or will the investigation be a bust?

Furthering our adventures in Argentina is the search for El Pombero, a prankster with a penchant for whistling and disrupting livestock. He is said to be a creature of vices, preferring tobacco, honey and rum as his chief source of sustenance. Perhaps he and the Tokoloshe should throw a milk n' honey party! Josh and the team see their invite, armed with offerings (bait) and whistle calls in an effort to flush out the pesky sprite.

Josh: "Yeah, he appears to have turned into a wolf, but still enjoys a tight pair of jeans. Like most men in Argentina. Y'know what I mean?"

Josh VO: "We found our first Waranee witness and local bar manager. Sort of a combination of Rosie O'Donnell and Meat Loaf."

Season One Milestones:
- S1 E1 - Show premieres to the World

CHAPTER 2:
THE HOST

While *Destination Truth* wasn't completely about Josh Gates, since the other major components had to do with the mysteries that were hunted, the travels and his crew, you have to admit that he was likely the main reason you got into this show. You know I'm right!

If you want to know a lot more about Joshua Gates, aside from this book and his work on TV, you should definitely look into getting a copy of his book *Destination Truth: Memoirs of a Monster Hunter* for a more in-depth story. For now, here is more about Josh based off of quotes he gave you, the fans, from various *DT Fan Radio* specials! A timeline of all his major entertainment projects can be located in **Acknowledgements**.

On his education: "I went to Tufts University in Boston and I double-majored in archeology and drama. So I have dual degrees from there, and then I worked out of college, and a little bit in college, as an excavator at a site overseas on the coast of Israel. Then, you know, fell into television and travel hosting a little bit after that. So, I do have some background in archeology."

On how he got into acting: "I had done a little theater in high school and Tufts has a great theater, this beautiful theater in the round. A sunken in 360 degree stage, a really neat space. My freshman year at Tufts, I was kind of spotted by one of the drama professors who took an interest in me and put me in one of his shows. From that point on, I was doing a lot of drama stuff, worked with the Student Drama Organization there, and was President of that my Junior and Senior year."

DID YOU KNOW?

Josh appeared in the reality show *Flavor of Love* featuring rapper Flavor Flav. Josh was a waiter at The Magic Castle in Hollywood and lucked into the cameo role. Look for him in Season 2, Episode 10.

Josh on how to be popular in school without trying: "I also was fortunate enough that I had a car on campus. I always remember this, because my parents gave me this old hand-me-down Jeep and a lot of kids didn't have cars. Because I lived so close to the university, I wanted to be able to go home on the weekends, see my parents, check in on them and stuff. So I spent a lot of time, you know, carting friends around in my car. Freshman year, I was the guy with the car, which was a real asset."

On religion: "I was raised in a family where we went to an Episcopal church. I was baptized Episcopalian and for the most part, I went to Sunday school and stuff like that as a kid and then, you know, I'm kind of one of those, major holiday Christians, at this point. I go for Easter and Christmas services and…I'm certainly a very open-minded person. I think that the more that you travel, especially when you travel to places where some of the world's really great religions are in full force. When you travel to Buddhist countries and Islamic countries and Hindu countries, you start to…fundamentally feel a bit more open minded because you recognize that there's a lot of people around the world that aren't, in a lot of ways, worshipping along the same guidelines, and the same sort of messages of what religion is about and the same kind of penance of peace and kindness and all those sorts of things…I certainly go into religious ceremonies that we observe on the show with as much reverence as I can for the individuals and the beliefs that go into them."

Giving advice to a fan on *DT Fan Radio*, Ashley, who wanted to double-major in oceanography (and advice to fans with similar goals): "Look, I also think that the notion of combining oceanography and archeology is really smart. I think that some of the big discoveries that are going to be happening in this era of archeology are going to be happening in sub-sea archeology. It's really at the very beginning stages due to technology to actually get down to so many things that have yet to be excavated from the ocean floor. There are some universities in the country that have great programs that deal with oceanography and deal with archeology...in the meantime, you can always volunteer to work at excavations that are doing underwater archeology and if you are SCUBA certified, or you get SCUBA certified...the excavation that I worked at, which is the city of Caesarea in Israel, that's how I started there. They take volunteers, and if you can cover your airfare and a couple other things, you won't get paid for the summer, but you'll get a real hands-on education."

 DID YOU KNOW?

DT Fan Radio was where Josh Gates and Brad Kuhlman first announced Josh's book. Josh said he wishes he had taken the initial offer of help from a ghost writer. "It has been a truly awful experience, in the best way possible!"

About showing injuries and illnesses on *DT*: "I have been a proponent of as much vomiting as possible on *Destination Truth*, but Standards and Practices (censors) don't always agree with me."

Josh's love of scarves: "I'm not obsessed with scarves, but you know, they are kinda standard part of the adventurer kit, right? It's like, scarves are good for sopping up sweat...they can be used for all sorts of things. You can wrap one around your head when trying to keep radioactive Chernobyl dust out of your mouth, and you can wear them on camels when you're trying to avoid the stink of horrible camels, and they're a pretty multi-purpose tool to have out there."

On Josh's OCD-level hoarding of Frequent Flier Miles: "I went home [to his Massachusetts hometown of Manchester-by-the-Sea] recently…and my mother was like 'Why don't you just use some miles to come home?' And I was like 'What, are you crazy? I'm not using my miles, those are my miles!' I can't go using my miles!"

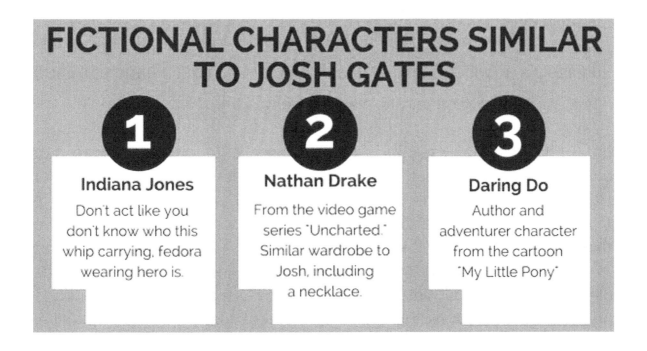

FICTIONAL CHARACTERS SIMILAR TO JOSH GATES

1
Indiana Jones
Don't act like you don't know who this whip carrying, fedora wearing hero is.

2
Nathan Drake
From the video game series "Uncharted." Similar wardrobe to Josh, including a necklace.

3
Daring Do
Author and adventurer character from the cartoon "My Little Pony"

Did Josh ever consider doing stand-up comedy? "I thought about doing stand-up but I'm not sure I have the nerve for it. Certainly when I was just sort of trying to hawk my wares as an actor, I was gravitating towards more comedic stuff and doing funnier, more sort of improv-y commercials. That was a world that I was, and am, interested in. I'm really happy that the show has provided a great outlet for not just my sense of humor, but the crew's sense of humor."

Was Josh ever considered as a celebrity cameo for any TV shows, back in the *DT* days? Josh became friends with Matt Nix, the Creator of *Burn Notice*, from working with him on a short film called *Singularity* (the fan site's name sake). Josh and Matt spoke about Josh appearing on *Burn*

Notice, but it sadly never happened. Josh was also considered as a celebrity guest star on Syfy's *Eureka*, but as show runner Bruce Miller said in an interview with the fan site, "one of the reasons we love them [potential celebrity guests] is that they are so good at their jobs. One of the reasons they are so good at their jobs is, or one of the results, is they're incredibly busy. Every time we want them on our show, it always ends up being a very difficult schedule problem." Recently, Zak Bagans of *Ghost Adventures* told the fan site via a Twitter Q&A that Josh is welcome on the paranormal show any time, which would certainly be awesome to see!

Does Josh believe any cryptids could be real? "In terms of unknown or cryptozoological animals out in the world, I think there are a few cases over the last few seasons of the show where I do genuinely believe that it's a real possibility. I think the Orang Pendek story we did in Indonesia, we certainly met a lot of credible researchers there - a National Geographic team, who feel as though there may be something uncatalogued in the jungles of Indonesia…I think there's a possibility that something could be going on there, and I think that some of the lake stories – I mean, not all of them, but some of them, where the lakes really could support life. There may be, you know, I'm sure they're not going to end up being enormous sea serpents, but there may be uncatalogued fauna in these lakes."

What's the one thing that Josh said on *DT Fan Radio* he would have left *DT* for, before his contract was up? "If they remade JAWS, I would just take a lawsuit from Syfy and just quit the channel completely." **What character would he be playing?** "I would be Hooper! …I'm not young [he likely meant old] enough to be Quint, right? He's kind of the old, salty seasoned veteran."

His taste in music: "Hesitantly I'm going to say, I'm kind of a big Country music fan. I know, it's devastating news for many listeners. Good Country though, not the junk, not the crappy pop, Top 40 Country. I do love Country and Bluegrass, so I listen to a lot of that. And I listen to a lot of, you know,

I guess the other stuff is less controversial is that I listen to Classic Rock and early Rock & Roll. I love The Beatles, I'm a big Beatles guy. And some 80's stuff, and that's about it...we'll often fight if there's a vehicle with an adapter that we can get the music out of the car and we'll sort of take turns. Everybody kind of gets a diplomacy of who gets to listen to what and when. So I feel like I'm at least getting exposed to a lot of different music."

If he were stuck on a deserted island, what would he want to bring?
"Obviously I'm going for the satellite phone and GPS locator and stuff like that. But if I am not allowed to get rescued and have to just make a life for myself on the island, I would think that I would want at least one really good book...a volleyball named Wilson, and a Nick's roast beef sandwich from Beverly, MA."

CHAPTER 3:
SEASON TWO

Our fandom with *Destination Truth* continued when Season Two was green-lit and aired on TV. With more episodes came more of the humor and cases we loved.

In Season 1, the intro script to the show was "I'm Josh Gates. My travels have taken me to the most exotic and mysterious places on earth. I've seen some unexplainable things which have raised some strange questions. Now, I've pulled together a crack team armed with the latest technology to search for answers. I'm not sure what's out there waiting for me, but I know what I'm looking for - the truth."

The intro animation for Season 1, which features the *DT* logo, showed the logo sitting on what looks like the horizon of a field or maybe an African plain, with the sun flaring behind it with shades of gold and purple as the sun appears to set to the right direction of the screen. The light noticeably highlights the second T in the word "truth." We saw this same animation for Season 2, but the intro script changed slightly:

"I'm Josh Gates. In my travels, I've seen some unexplainable things which have raised strange questions. Now I've pulled together a team armed with the latest technology in the search for answers. I'm not sure what's out there waiting for me, but I know what I'm looking for - the truth."

Season 2, Episode 1
Destination: Nepal
Case: Yeti
Original Air Date: March 5th, 2008

The Yeti is one of the most famous creatures in cryptozoology, often classified as their big trinity, in the same popularity of the Sasquatch and the Loch Ness monster. The beast is commonly known by the misnomer of "The Abominable Snowman" and makes it's home in the great Himalayan peaks of the Bhutan and Tiber regions of Southern Asia. The creature is often considered a near sacred entity by local Tibetan monks and the local native population have told tales of its existence for centuries.

Josh's search for the Yeti expands into *DT*'s first full episode investigation. They travel deep into the Kathmandu region and have a near violent confrontation with not a creature, but with an angry monk in a Monastery that houses an alleged Yeti artifact.

Traveling deeper into the freezing peaks of Mount Everest, the team continues their hunt for one of the most intriguing and promising cryptids in the annals of *Destination Truth*.

Fun fact: The evidence collected from this particular episode is on display for fans to see in the line queue of *Expedition Everest* at Disney's Animal Kingdom in Orlando, Florida.

FUNNY QUOTES THIS EPISODE

Josh VO: "Landing a 30-year-old prop plane in the middle of a mountain range is a lot like the backside of a Yeti - a little hairy."

Josh: "You know, regular stuff. You got your pens, duct tape, night vision scopes." **Brad**: "If we catch a Yeti, we're gonna duct tape him to the tree, somewhere maybe." **Josh**: "Yeah."

Season 2, Episode 2
Destinations: Pemba Island & the Gobi Desert
Cases: Haunted African Island & Mongolian Death Worm
Original Air Date: March 12th, 2008

The world of the paranormal can be described many ways, but rarely can one label it as "punctual". Our team's next investigation takes them to a haunted village on the African island of Pemba, in the Zanzibar archipelago. Here, the spirits of the past are said to congregate at the stroke of midnight around a mystical tree.

Team Truth witnesses a tribal ceremony and encounters possible possessions, and would-be animal sacrifices, en route to uncovering the mystery. Will they make the midnight deadline or will the team miss out on witnessing the ghostly graveyard shift?

Next, within the vast expanse of the Gobi Desert, there is said to exist a creature with the colorful moniker of the Mongolian Death Worm. Known locally as Olgoi-Khorkoi, the creepy crawly is essentially a super-powered, 3 to 4 foot annelid. It is said to possess the abilities to spew acid and to emit an electric charge, but no word on if it can leap tall sand dunes with a single bound (*Beetlejuice* reference, FYI).

Braving the adversities of failing equipment and sub-zero temperatures, Josh and the *DT* crew dig deep to find the worm's lair. Where are Kevin Bacon and Michael Gross from *Tremors* when you need them?

Josh: "In-flight movie?" **Pilot**: "Some turbulence, maybe." **Josh**: "Turbulence? Perfect." **Josh VO**: "A sudden problem with the plane's fuel pump negated our plans and threatened to turn our short flight over the ruins into an all new season of *Lost*." **Josh (upon landing safely)**: "You don't see that [expletive] on *Ghost Hunters*. EVER."

Josh: "This is exactly what Christmas looks like at my house."

Josh VO: "The drive seemed like a breeze at first. Sure, the scenery was a little spartan, but at least the highway was paved. Until it wasn't."

Season 2, Episode 3
Destinations: Cambodia &
Republic of the Congo
Cases: Wild Man & Mokele Mbembe
Original Air Date: March 19th, 2008

Feral humans do not specifically classify as cryptids, as they have been proven a real phenomena. People who have been said to have spirited away to the wild regress to a primal and animalistic state. They have been popularized by such fictional accounts as *The Jungle Book*, *Tarzan* and the myth of Romulus and Remus, not to mention many true life accounts.

Team Truth encounters a girl in Cambodia, who has said to have recently returned from a long-term disappearance into the wild. No longer possessing the ability to speak, the team attempts to communicate with her with help from her family and reveal the identity of her primal throwback suitor.

As we have seen, alleged living dinosaurs are amongst the most enduring and prevalent of crypto mysteries. Mokele Mbembe AKA "He Who Stops the Flow of the River" is amongst the most well known, prevalent in popular culture and with many well-funded expeditions dispatched to uncover it. The rivers and swamps of the Congo are said to be the habitat of this sauropodian beast, a Jurassic relic that doesn't need an amber-infused mosquito to still walk the Earth.

Josh and his team embark on an aquatic expedition, braving the documented dangers of the African marsh in an effort to locate this age-old Mesozoic mystery.

Josh VO: "We flew across the Pacific [Ocean] to Phnom Penh, the capital of Cambodia, where we met up with the rest of our crew. Our luggage, on the other hand, went somewhere else entirely." **T-Bone**: "There's a lot of things that are gonna hurt us, if we don't get that gear." **Josh**: "That's not good." **Ponch**: "I don't have a boom pole!" **Josh**: "You don't have a boom pole?! I don't have a pair of underwear!" **Ponch**: "That sucks. Glad I got my stuff!" **Josh**: "What a team player."

Josh VO: "He even offered to take us in his boat." (After some time, once everyone is in the boat) **Josh**: "One pull. Two pulls. Three pulls. Four pulls. That's five. Six pulls - he's priming it - seven. Eight pulls! We're up on eight! Annnd our motor's dead."

Season 2, Episode 4
Destinations: Vietnam & East Africa
Cases: Tarasque & Popobawa
Original Air Date: March 26th, 2008

Halong Bay in Hanoi, Vietnam has its very own aquatic enigma. The Tarasque holds roots in French culture but has seemingly migrated to this South Eastern Asian locale. Its serpentine form has been inspiring both fear in local fishing villages and plenty of bad puns from Josh Gates.

Fish-finding sonar and SCUBA gear are the tools that aid the crew in their dive into the murky waters of the bay. A kayak expedition into the local flooded caverns intensifies the adventure in the quest for the truth to Vietnam's very own Nessie.

One of the most unusual creatures investigated by *DT* comes next, as the Popobawa is said to be a bat-like, cyclops menace that emits a bioluminescent light. It is also one of the most reportedly aggressive cryptids yet, as witnesses attest to being physically assaulted in their homes at night.

Stone Town, Zanzibar is the venue for a night time sky scan. Odd political leanings to the mystery further compound the sightings, making this one of the most bizarre investigations for Team Truth.

Josh VO: "After a quick hoop session with the undergrads, there was also no question that I posed no threat in the NBA draft." **Josh**: "Little short, a little short, a little short! Bah!" (Makes basket after five throws) **Josh**: "That's how it's done! That's how we do it! 300 tries to get that take."

Ponch: "You got enough Dong?" **Josh**: "I got a lot of Dong. The currency in this country is about as out of control as I've ever seen a currency. There are 16,000 Dong to one [American] dollar."

Josh: "How much for the whole thing?" **Vendor**: "20,000 shillings." **Josh**: "It's a good deal. Looks fresh. Not a lot of flies on it, which is good."

Another of the more unusual beasts on our itinerary, the Mapinguari has traits that represent both the fantastical and natural, depending on which witness you interview. According to Amazonian lore, the beast is a large, hairy creature with a single eye and a mouth centered on its stomach. Facing the real natural dangers of the Amazon, Josh and team set off into the dark rainforest to locate the massive mystery creature.

Then, the Kongamato, translated to "The Breaker of Boats", is a pterosaur-like beast which has been allegedly terrorizing the swamps of the Congo for years. First being reported to the Western world in the 1920's, perhaps it is related to the Ropen, with a notable exception of preferring live human flesh as opposed to cadavers.

Josh and the team set off into Africa to scan the skies in search of this leather-winged predator. Following their earlier hunt in the same region for the Mokele Mbembe, will the team uncover a true-life *Lost World*?

Josh VO: "Tales of the Mapinguari are pervasive…what everyone agrees on, though, is that he stinks to high hell. Emitting a pungent odor when he's in the vicinity. Kind of like my crew by the end of our trip."

Josh: "We got one car with the hood up already." **Brad**: "Which is never a good sign!" **Josh**: "Which only means we'll be on the side of the road in ten minutes." **Brad**: "Pretty much par for the course, Gates!" **Josh:** "Pretty much part of the experience on *Destination Truth*."

Season 2, Episode 6
Destination: Brazil
Case: Giant Anaconda
Original Air Date: April 9th, 2008

In this special hour-long investigation, Josh is joined by Jennifer Lopez, Ice Cube and David Hasselhoff in a quest to scour the Amazon for a fabled giant snake. Okay, only part of that is true, but could you imagine the ratings?

The concept of a 30-foot-long snake is determined biologically possible, as anacondas are the largest snakes in the world and specimens of about 20 feet in length have been discovered.

Perils of the Amazon await, including smaller, but no less deadly, predatory serpents. Will Josh discover evidence of a massive snake, or will the investigation, like the film franchise the snake inspired, emerge a bomb?

Josh VO: "The doctor agreed to take me into a pit of live anacondas at the

Institute. All I needed now was a fedora and a whip." **Josh**: "These guys need my help? The more, the merrier? Or am I just gonna get in the way and get my face bit off?...I tell you what I need - I need to be on *Battlestar Galactica* and get off of this crazy show!"

Josh: "Yeah, I'm gonna try it and it's gonna be embarrassing, like it always is every time I do this on the show. Any tips for me?" **Translator**: "He says not to hit the camera guy." **Josh**: "He's funny. Can you tell him he's got a job as a comedian?"

Season 2, Episode 7
Destinations: Australia & Malaysia
Cases: Yowie & Haunted Mosque
Original Air Date: September 3rd, 2008

This investigation is a landmark for Team Truth. Utilizing the talents of Ping Pong Productions and their creature creation software for the first time, the team makes their inaugural Australian investigation. Joined for the first time by fan-favorite Erin Ryder, the team sets off into the outback to investigate the continent's own resident hairy hominid.

Australia is one of the few continents with absolutely no native simians, let alone great apes, so what are the locals seeing? Will Team Truth discover the identity of Bigfoot's cousin as they trek into the land down under?

Team Truth then heads to Malaysia to explore an abandoned mosque, feared by the locals for tales of alleged angry phantoms. Stories tell of a frightening, long haired female spirit that only appears to men and causes physical discomfort to all who witness her. With chilling isolation sessions in the mosque, will the *DT* crew experience what goes bump in the Malayasian night?

Josh VO: "Long story short, we needed climbing and trekking gear." **Josh**: "Am I like Van Helsing?" **Josh VO**: "Since we were already shopping, I thought I'd try my luck at a new hat." **Ryder:** "Oh, um, you know, it's like a wedding dress - you don't wanna go with the first one you try on." **Josh:** "Fair enough."

Josh: "Oh my God, that's the worst thing I've ever tasted!" **Jarrod**: "I like 'em!" **Josh**: "It tastes like a dirty mackerel peed in my mouth."

Josh VO: "We met up with a paranormal researcher named Uncle. Yes, his name is 'Uncle'." **Josh**: "Do many locals believe this mosque is haunted?" **Uncle**: "Yes, yes. So many things are weird. Ghosts, or locals call it Pontianak - they're like bitches." **Josh**: "Bitches?" **Uncle**: "Yes." (Josh gives incredulous look to camera) **Josh**: "Banshees?" **Uncle**: "Banshees!" **Josh**: "Not bitches. Banshees. That's very different." **Uncle**: "Oh my God! Banshees, okay."

Season 2, Episode 8
Destinations: Indonesia & Iceland
Cases: Orang Pendek & Lagarfljót Worm
Original Air Date: September 10th, 2008

Sumatra is an Asian island famed for it's populace of great apes known as Orangutans. However, if locals are to be believed, there may be a larger and more enigmatic hominid lurking in their forests. The Orang Pendek is said to be a relatively small, ranging from three to five feet in height.

The island is vastly unexplored, leaving plenty of ample landscape for the team to venture into. Josh (AKA "White Rice," his newly adopted rap alter ego from this episode) and team venture into the uncharted wilderness.

Then, Team Truth journeys into the tundras of Iceland to find the Lagarfljót. Said to be a massive, worm-like water creature that spans the length of a full football field or larger, it has been reported since the 12th century with roots in Viking and Scandinavian folklore.

A particularly perilous journey takes the team onto the near frozen waters of Lake Lagarfljót. With unfriendly temperatures, heavy fog and the possibility of becoming a lake creature's dinner, the team has their work cut out for them in more ways than one.

Josh: "Never easy. This. Show. Is. Never. Easy!"

Merchant: "Try something really Icelandic. And this makes you a man." **Josh**: "Okay. First of all, you're saying I'm not a man yet. Not sure I like your tone, ma'am." **Merchant**: "This is sour testicles." **Josh**: "Wait, what? Why? Oh, boy." **Merchant**: "This, is better to eat first and then I'll tell you." **Josh**: "No, no, I don't play that game."

Season 2, Episode 9
Destinations: Indonesia & Australia
Cases: Haunted Jakarta Cave & Burrunjor
Original Air Date: September 17th, 2008

Deep in Indonesia, there exists a waterlogged cave purportedly haunted by the spirits of the past. Locals fear to tread here, as the spirits are said to be very unfriendly to visitors. Josh and the team employ a local guide and a medium in an attempt to communicate with the spectral spelunkers. Disembodied voices and mysterious shadows haunt the team as they brave natural dangers and creepy crawlies in the depths of the cavern. All this adds up to a particularly perilous journey into the unknown.

Then, we journey back to the Outback as Josh investigates sightings of a creature etched in Aboriginal lore. While not quite an alleged living dinosaur, the Burrunjor is said to be a massive reptilian creature, similar to the therapod class of thunder lizards. Prelavant in the continent's Northern Territory region and it is a scourge on the local livestock. The DT Crew must stay off the menu themselves, as they hunt for this mystery predator.

Josh: "Ma'am, this is gross. This is the grossest market of all time. What is this? You have, like, Harry Potter animals in here!"

Josh VO: "When we landed, Ryder complained of dizziness. Worried that she was suffering from dehydration in the extreme heat, I had our medic Jarrod check her out." **Josh**: "If we could just get her over to the investigation site, she can kind of hang back there while we set stuff up." **Casey**: "Yeah." **Josh**: "Or we can shoot her. Put her down." **Casey**: "One less person. Trim the fat." **Ryder**: "I can hear you, idiots!"

Season 2, Episode 10
Destinations: Indonesia & Philippines
Cases: Ahool & Pinatubo Monster
Original Air Date: September 24th, 2008

Flying cryptids and Indonesian anomalies are familiar ground for Team DT, so it was inevitable that the two would eventually come together. Their next investigation takes them back to Jakarta to seek this bat-like beast with a very distinctive cry,hence its namesake. The Ahool is said to have a wingspan of up to 10 feet and tends to stalk both the forests and caves of the region.

Locals fear the waters of this region in the Phillipines, the alleged lair of an eight foot carnivorous water monster, which is our next case. Both fear of the beast and authentic leaks of deadly mercury from a local mine in the water have put a halt on the local fishing economy. Tales of a sunken city in the region present plenty of hiding places for the beast as well.

With these dangers in mind, the team bravely plunges into the depths in an effort to rid the locals of their fear. Will Josh go mad as a hatter in the poisonous waters of the Mapanuepe Lake, or will he uncover the identity of this aquatic menace?

Josh VO: "As usual, our military-grade night vision cameras were a hit at customs and part of our crew got held up at the airport trying to explain that we were just here to hunt monsters."

Ryder: "You know what I think?" **Josh**: "Yes?" **Ryder**: "I think you rented this thing from a couple of A-holes."

Season 2, Episode 11
Destinations: Japan & the Philippines
Cases: Aokigahara Forest & Aswang
Original Air Date: October 1st, 2008

At the base of Mount Fuji lies Aokigahara Forest, which boasts the beautiful nickname "The Sea of Trees," as well as the more sinister nickname "The Suicide Forest". This 14-mile-wide labyrinth is infamous for an unusually high suicide amount - so much so, that suicide prevention postings are a regular sight amongst the trails. With so much pain and despair embedded beneath the canopy, the forest is a haven for spirits known as the Yurei.

The team sets off into the trails in search of these phantoms. Disquieting experiences follow with a sense of general unease, coupled with chilling video footage, and you have the making of one of *DT*'s most haunting expeditions yet.

Then, the Aswang, AKA Tik-Tik, is a powerful and well known being of Filipino mythology. The name itself is Sanskrit for "demon" and the fiend holds no definitive shape, as it can take on a myriad of forms. They can even take on human form and often indulge in their diet of human organs. These terrifying spectres have been popularized in Western culture, thanks to popular fiction like Grimm and Supernatural.

Josh and the crew venture to an isolated village in the Phillipines to investigate a local church said to be haunted by a rash of Aswang sightings. **Special note**: This is the infamous "Balut" investigation, in which the team indulges in perhaps the most unsettling foreign delicacy we have ever seen on *DT*.

Josh VO: "Traveling internationally means that sometimes, you have to trust pictures to interpret for you." **Josh**: "To my knowledge, you do not read Japanese. How do you know this is cooling eye drops?" **Casey**: "It had an eye on the cup." **Josh VO**: "But there are some things you shouldn't leave to chance." **Josh**: "Son of a, God! I'm a pirate now. Casey, your eye drops turned me into a pirate." **Casey**: "Arrr!"

Josh: "Is there a nude, Japanese cowboy anywhere nearby? Stop stealing people's clothes!"

Josh: "Sir, I know we have a language barrier in our cultures, but your boat is sinking."

DID YOU KNOW? Nick Groff, formerly of *Ghost Adventures* and currently in the show *Paranormal Lockdown*, was quite a fan of *DT* when it was on the air. While he couldn't tell you every episode by heart, he did have a favorite. He said to the fan site during a 2012 podcast that "I watched a couple of his shows [episodes]. It's cool. You know which one I actually dug a lot? It was when he went to Russia, and he went to…the nuclear power plant that exploded and it wiped out the whole town and everything [Chernobyl]. The only reason I saw that is because I was researching that location a year prior to them going there with my cousin Justin. We were looking at that (location) because I really wanted to take *GA* there, and I was like 'aw, we'll never be able to get this - it's so hard and complicated.' Then, I see Josh go there, and I was so fascinated!"

Season 2, Episode 12
Destinations: Japan & Iceland
Cases: Issie & Elves
Original Air Date: October 8th, 2008

Lake Ikeda in Southern Japan plays host to a lake monster all its own. Issie is said to be a 30 to 40 foot humped creature, similar both in appearance, and marketing opportunities, to its famous Scottish cousin, Nessie. Issie is a boon both to local pop culture, going so far as to inspire a character from the Pokemon franchise, and to the more spiritual side of the region.

Local Shinto lore decrees the lake as a cradle of civilization, crediting Issie as a potential harbinger of mankind. Josh and his team seek scientific, natural answers to the beast's identity and launch another aquatic investigation.

Josh earns his long sought after elf hunting license in the second half of the episode's unique investigation! Elves are much more than cookie bakers, Will Ferrell movies or dolls used to keep children in line during the holidays. In fact, they actually hold deep cultural relevance, especially to the people of Iceland. On this European island, more than half of the population believe in the little people and are willing to even alter their own cityscape to protect the diminutive creatures.

Sights set on science, Josh and the team venture to the Icelandic forests and hills, with this expedition being a perfect showcase to prove that no matter how outlandish a case may be, the team is willing to view evidence and uncover any shred of truth that there is to be discovered.

Josh: "I'd like to welcome you aboard our transport. I'll be doing karaoke for the next four hours. If you have any requests, please let me know. There is no smoking here, in the doily van. These beautiful doilies were handmade in the 15th century, specifically for this van."

Josh: "So Casey? Just so I get this straight - we're looking for elves?" **Casey**: "This is correct. Elves." **Josh**: "There was never a point in my life where I thought, 'one day, I'll take a crew of people, boxes of technology, night vision scopes, thermal imagers, and I will hunt those elves.' I never thought that day would come, but it's here!"

Season 2, Episode 13
Destinations: West Africa - The Gambia
Cases: Ninki Nanka & Kikiyaon
Original Air Date: October 15th, 2008

The Ninka Nanka is a West African cryptid said to resemble a classic dragon (minus the wings) and is amphibious in nature. The horned beast is feared as a dangerous carnivore and often used as a boogeyman to frighten young children. Team Truth travels to the tiny country known as The Gambia and embark on a marsh-based hunt.

Far removed from the usual bat and bird-like cryptids, the Kikiyaon is said to be virtually a man/owl hybrid, in the following case. The local tribes of The Gambia, no doubt still reeling from alleged dragon attacks, fear the avian menace and appease it through dance and ceremony. Continuing their African adventure, Team Truth sets off into the wild plains amongst the perils and danger of a hyena pack roving the area. They must keep one eye in the air and another on the ground during their nocturnal hunt for this horrific hooter.

Josh: "I mean, every piece of gear on that list is essential for me to conduct my spying operations here in Gambia. How did they catch on?"

Josh: "I almost stepped on a crocodile. I gotta get my [expletive] together."

Season Two Milestones:

- **S2 E1** - First episode focusing on only one case/investigation
- **S2 E7** - Creature building software with 3D animations during case review premieres and first Mid-Season premiere (April to September spent editing the second half of Season)
- **S2 E11** - Josh meets President of the Philippines and the crew helps with local recovery efforts after local typhoon

CHAPTER 4:
DT CREW

One of the biggest elements that fans enjoyed about *Destination Truth*, and one common note of feedback for fans in regards to Josh's newer series *Expedition Unknown*, is that we got to see him work alongside his fearless crew (list of cast members is located in **Acknowledgements**).

"We really think that building a team dynamic is an important part of the show," Josh said of the fellow cast members he worked with, on an old episode of *DT Fan Radio*. "We certainly try to highlight all the comedic and dramatic moments that happen out there, and make that a part of the show."

"A group of people that can kind of survive the months on the road, keep a great disposition and work hard," Josh said in a separate *DT Fan Radio* special about the caliber of people he works with. "The thing about *DT*, we always say this, is that there's so few people on the crew and it is such a lean group, that everybody end ups pulling, you know, double duty, triple duty, and they really do a lot more than their job definition on paper."

Team Truth was a group of audio, video, medical and research-related experts that rotated each season who joined in on the fear and the funnies. While we loved Josh's humor and his sense of authority, it was fun when his cast mates took him down a couple of notches from time-to-time, especially in regards to one of Josh's more beloved sidekicks, Erin Ryder.

"We're like a big, stupid family when we're out on the road," Erin Ryder told fans in a *DT Fan Radio* interview in 2012. "Long car trips - you'll see the best and worst of everyone. I think we had a lot of fun in Kazakhstan. I think it was one of those locations where it was so easy to be fun, silly and by that time, we had all really gotten to know each other…but I think it's just getting to be out there and travel with this great group of people."

"I can't say that there was one really great moment…I have a problem picking favorites all together," Ryder said during the interview, on her favorite moment being on *DT*. "But this season [Season 5] was up there in the tops, for me." Ryder has described herself on *DT Fan Radio* as "a big jock" and said that she's worked on MTV, Cartoon Network and many other projects, including the show *Chasing UFOs*, but she said that "my heart will always be with *DT*."

"I got involved with *DT* during their prep for season 3.0," Evan B. Stone said in an email interview with the fan site. "I just got off a five year job as a Director for Al Gore's Emmy Award winning documentary channel doing social issue documentaries and was ready for something adventurous."

"I've always been into the unexplained, and especially ancient aliens and all things strange and scary, so the chance at traveling the world was perfect for me at the time," Evan stated. "The interview was all about, 'Are you okay with sleeping in creepy places?' Yes. 'Are you okay with skipping a meal once a while?' Yes. 'Long hours?' Yes. 'Are you afraid of anything?' YES, BUGS! Oh well, time to face my fears. Side note: All caves have creepy bugs with big eyes!"

"I don't think it really sunk in that I was part of this team until I boarded the first of those 30 flights we took," Ali Zubik from Season 4 said in an interview with the fan site back in 2010 via email. "I found that a sleep mask, iPod, and sticking my frozen feet under Mike Morrell's armpits all help do the trick, though."

Every crew member serves a vital function to the crew, and the medics of the show have definitely been very important to the team. Shawn Goodwin and Rex Williams have sat down with the fan site a few times to talk about their experiences.

"I spent seven years in the military in the United States Navy," Shawn said on an episode of *DT Fan Radio*, when speaking of his medical background. "I was a Corpsman, and that involves going to a basic Corps School in Chicago, then a list of more technical, surgical schools. I also have Special Operations experience with deployments, and I've deployed with Special Ops units in Iraq. Deployed multiple other places on a multitude of trauma and emergency medical skill sets all over the world."

"We're in this third world country and the emergency room is a dirt floor with a straw hut," Shawn continued, painting a picture of what a set medic job is like on *DT*. "My backpack and my skill set are usually what the best choice is."

Entities-R-Us

Entities-R-Us

Entities-R-Us

"I've spent a little over six years of just working full time as a medic and on an ambulance, working 24 hours, 48 hours, 72 hours straight, sometimes even 96 hours straight on an ambulance without going home," Rex Williams told fans of his medical experience before *DT*. He said that a good day of filming for the show was "when I don't have to use my medic skills - that's a good day!"

"The worst injury - we've had a few, luckily nothing too serious," Rex revealed. "We haven't had any broken bones yet, knock on wood. We've had bumps and bruises, scrapes, and Josh kind of scraped up his leg in China when we were doing the Yeren episode…Gabe took a spill off a horse in Season Three in the Andes mountains, injured his knee, but it wasn't dislocated or broken."

"I would think the worst thing that comes to mind was off-camera that was actually our last day in Chile, this last season," Rex shared, when thinking of the worst *DT* injury he treated. He told the story of how his fellow cast used some downtime to go surfing and an unfortunate event Gabe had.

"He actually stepped on a bed of sea urchins and got a bunch of their spines imbedded in his foot and in his legs. It was pretty hardcore, man, he stepped right on it and said it was like stepping in pin cushions…luckily, they weren't poisonous."

Rex continued "The barbs, the spines, they have little barbs on them so when they go in, they tend to not wanna come out. So I had to actually go in with a scalpel and dig each spine out of his foot, the bottom of his feet. It took about four hours to do. He had about 13 spines in his feet, and the last one, was the worst one I saved for last. It was really deep in his foot and I actually had to make an incision…I had to give him a little local anesthetic to numb it up and go in. I gave him an IV and some antibiotics prophylactically to ward away any infection. He recovered a few weeks later and he was fine. I think that'd be the worst one."

What does the crew do if the medic is down for the count? "Everybody on the show is pretty well versed with basic emergency medicine," Shawn says. "Anytime we go out, I will study in-depth all of the indigenous dangers of the area and kind of give everybody a heads up of the stuff I have available to me in my bag that it's kind of common knowledge anybody can use. Stuff like the tourniquets, the EpiPen, stuff like that."

"When I was in high school, I did small movies with my friends, skateboard videos and whatnot," Gabe Copeland said on *DT Fan Radio* about how he got started in filming. "Then, I moved down to Los Angeles about 13 years ago and I kinda started acting a little bit. Through college, I studied television and film, and I was always a photographer. Then I just started loading film on smaller movies, then worked on different things. Now, I'm in reality [TV], still doing films and whatnot, so yeah, now I'm here, doing *DT*."

"Basically, a producer called me and you just go in for an interview, and you had to be on camera for this job, which was a little different," Gabe recalls, of how he got on *DT* in the first place. "So they had to interview me on camera. A lot of other guys would come and show up, and they started talking about where we were going and what we were shooting, and I started getting into it. They liked me, so I set sail for my first Season, which was 2.5 for me, and they asked me to come back for Season 3.0, so I did that one, too!"

FUNNY CREW QUOTE: **Josh**: "Gabe, why is there a giant statue of you in Kiev?" **Gabe**: "I've been here before and they knew of my greatness." - **Season 3, Episode 4**

"Travel, research, monster hunting - Who could turn that down? " Sharra Jenkins-Romany, the tech manager for the Season 3 crew, told me in 2010 via email. Her story is definitely very unique in the *DT* tapestry.

"At the time, I was a camera operator on a VH1 Reality show in Los Angeles," Sharra said, "and we were just two weeks into a five-week run, but when *DT* came a-knockin', I gave notice and left to join the crew."

Luckily for her, this decision put her on the path for the adventure of a lifetime, in more ways than one. "Being a part of *DT* was an experience I'll never forget. Not just because of the amazing journey…but because it is where I met my husband, Ramy Romany."

"I feel fortunate to have had the opportunity to see the world, and do the job I love, just before falling in love and starting a family," Sharra concluded. "You really could not have asked for a better scenario."

"Obviously, *Destination Truth* was a life changer. I met Sharra on that," Ramy Romany, the English-accented Egyptian fixer we encountered in Season 3, said on *DT Fan Radio*. "She's the love of my life and my wife forever, and the mother of my baby, so *DT* comes first, or else my wife isn't going to like it if I say anything else."

Ramy said in the interview that Bicha had worked with him before on another project and recommended him to Josh, and that's how the relationship began. It is worthwhile to mention that when he did this interview, it was at a tumultuous time.

"From my side of the world, my country fell apart and I have no government, at the moment," he said, recounting in early 2011 when there was huge civil unrest in Egypt. "My President finally resigned and gave up, which is kind of a good and bad thing. No one knows what's gonna happen.

The situation was pretty bad when I decided to take Sharra and my baby, and leave."

Ramy continued to reminisce on the situation, saying "Cairo is one of these really safe cities. The people are all friendly and the tradition is people are safe…with these unfortunate events, it's been turned into a lawless city. It was so bad. I was driving with Sharra and Sophia, my daughter, in the back seat, and on the streets, there were these big people with big weapons, swords and guns on the streets."

During the time of the interview, he spoke of the horrors that had become of Cairo and was concerned that he heard the Mask of King Tut had been stolen during rioting, and feared that whoever stole it would melt it down to steal the gold. Fortunately, the mask has since been recovered and restored, but there has been controversy as of January of 2016 where museum employees will be charged with negligence, after there were issues with the restoration process.

"There wasn't passion, at the beginning," Ramy told us, of his experience in production fixing. "I started when I was 13 years old. I was basically a spoiled brat - my father started this 30 years ago and I wanted to be on location, just like any kid…it was just a cool thing to be around." Ramy handled AKA fixed his first project at age 13 for BBC TV. "I had the contacts and I would just go out to the Pyramids of Giza and say 'Hello, Mister General Manager of Giza! Could you let us film here? It'll be fine.' Everyone would speak to me as their son, rather than a client or someone who wants to work with them."

He and Sharra, still together, have been splitting their time between the USA and traveling to film. They were even nominated for two Emmys for a documentary they worked on called *Heritage* in 2015.

In an interview with Troy Tackett, who reviewed evidence for Season 2 episodes, he shared some intel on his role with the show. He had blown it off, at first, and then when Megan from Ping Pong called, he said "what the hell's this *Destination Truth* stuff and who keeps calling me to do this analysis stuff?...I just thought it was some crank calls, like someone messing with me."

For Season 3, Troy did the EVP analysis, but someone else was on screen to review it. He spoke of a specific, amusing piece of evidence shared in the Icelandic Elves episode that Troy found via EVP. "I still get a kick out of it, every time I watch that episode... it was funny that day, when we were shooting in the studio."

FUNNY CREW QUOTE: **Josh**: "Bobby, what are you doing?" **Bobby**: "Calling in the calls on bear-talkie." **Josh**: "Did you just steal a child's toy, gut it, and put a walkie-talkie inside of it?" **Bobby**: "No. I stole Vanessa's toy, gutted it, and put a walkie-talkie inside of it." - **Season 4, Episode 1**

"Well, you know, I grew up with my father being a photographer and he, I guess, gave me a lot of insight," Jael de Pardo said on a *DT Fan Radio* episode, as to her filming roots. "I was very intrigued with, like, visual art and after a few years, I decided that I wanted to study some art. I actually went to school in Manhattan at an art school called The Fashion Institute of Technology, and I studied multimedia arts. I had some friends who were making films and I was studying photography, and I just became really interested in it."

FUNNY FACT

Rex pranked Jael when she was doing a *DT Fan Radio* show with me. This occurred on the May 2010 interview with her and it was hilarious.

"When we're on the road for *Destination Truth*, we are literally, we hit the ground running and it is a nonstop thing," Jael continued. "I mean, we barely have a moment, you know, to ourselves. Its kinda wild, I mean it's like we absolutely become family out there because we're out there 24/7 and we're always on the go."

"I didn't really get to collect too much stuff, unfortunately," Jael told fans, when asked if she had any cool keepsakes on her *DT* travels. "Maybe like just a few stickers to put on my bike. You know, on my fridge or like a magnet to at least say, okay look, I was in Egypt."

"It's different everywhere we go, to be honest with you," Shawn said, when asked how often they get to shower when doing *DT*. "We never really know what to expect, so far as lodging or travel. Sometimes in the airport, you land and you take a bird bath in the airport, you change your clothes really quick, and then that's what you get. Sometimes, you're in a marble shower. It's literally wherever you go."

FUNNY CREW QUOTE: **Ryder**: "How are we gonna split up the million dollars, when we find the mermaid?" **Josh**: "Split it? What are you talking about? I get a million dollars, and you all get a free trip to Kiryat Yam, Israel." **Ryder**: "The math seems faulty." **Josh**: "We have 48 hours to find this mermaid, get the money and get out of town. Basically the plot of *Oceans 11*." **Ryder**: "Thank God [that] Rex is a Chinese acrobat." - **Season 3, Episode 11**

"We have a research period that we do in our offices in Los Angeles and typically it's about anywhere from four to eight weeks, depending on how many episodes are ordered," Brad Kuhlman said on *DT Fan Radio* a few years back. "We spend that time, you know, finding the stories that we're going to cover, finding local people in the countries we're going to, to sort of aid us in our trip there."

"It's a bit of a jigsaw puzzle, trying to put a trip like that together," Brad continued. "It's a bunch of countries, one after the other, and it's a lot of travel. It's about six weeks, actually."

"It costs a lot of money to go out on the road, be out there and travel to all those places," Brad said to fans, continuing on the difficulties of filming. "To stay the night, and get local assistance and you know, pay Josh Gates' salary." That quote certainly drew a hearty laugh from Josh, who was on the same *DT Fan Radio* special, at the time.

It's unbelievable to think about it, but there was actually a show that was more insane to work on for Brad than *DT*. "*Jerry Springer* was the craziest thing there ever was. Listen, *DT* is crazy in its own way. It's crazy hard and sometimes, you can't believe you are where you are and it takes you to insane places. *Springer* was, I don't know - the people you interact with on a daily basis on that show, it was a head scratcher every day there."

FUNNY QUOTE: **Josh**: "You know how many crew members we've lost to the Hare Krishna over the years? A LOT." **Bobby**: "Mike's got sweet dance maneuvers, too." **Josh**: "Gonna miss that guy." -Season 3, Episode 13

"The world is a big place and I guess anything is possible," Shawn said, back in 2010 on *DT Fan Radio*, about his paranormal beliefs. He, like Josh Gates, remains an open-minded skeptic. Meanwhile, *DT* seems to have swayed another crew member very much.

"The paranormal is a serious business - I've always felt that way," Ali told me during our 2010 email interview. "There is something to it that cannot be denied, and working on this show really confirmed what I had always thought."

Brad said on *DT Fan Radio* of his belief in cryptids, that "Of all the stories that we've covered, the Yeti is probably, you know, [its] got the best shot to be a real guy. It could be a real animal."

Gabe says of the paranormal that he is "Pretty skeptical, probably more so than the other guys, but I am definitely open minded and I feel like there's definitely something out there."

"I'm not sure if we know anything about it and, you know, these people believe in these mysteries," Gabe assesses of his beliefs versus those of other cultures in these paranormal cases. "These aren't just made up - they're passed down through generations, so we're kind of searching out the myth, seeing if there's any validity to it. I don't know if this has added to or taken away from what I believe in."

Gabe said that one of his scariest events was filming in the Suicide Forest. "That was such a real thing to me that I'll never forget that…it actually kind of touched me." The second scariest thing, to him, was a real-life threat. "I also almost got bitten by a viper in Indonesia, so both of those two things, I never really forget."

Does Gabe believe in the paranormal being able to mess with filming gear? "Electronics can malfunction at any time, so you don't really know," he said. "I really doubt it, but you never know!" If you want to see some cool photographs Gabe has done in his travels, which includes his *DT* treks, check them out at *GabrielCopelandPhotography.com*

On one of the most iconic episodes, in which the crew goes back to the Hoia Baciu forest, Ryder recalls what it was like to shoot it and how the final product came out. "I think it couldn't have been better than going back to the haunted forest with Evan, so I was really excited that we came out of the gate with that. I think it came out really well, and everyone was really happy with it."

"Bringing him (Evan) back to the haunted forest was something we were all really excited but nervous about," Ryder continued. "You want to make sure that everyone is safe, and he definitely put himself up for it. We had no idea what was going to happen with going back there…we just wanted to go back and see what we could find ourselves."

On the incident that lead to Evan's ears to bleed, Ryder said "He thinks he might have re-injured an old injury. The nerves and the pressure, all that kind of resulted in that, but it was a scary moment for all of us. I think you don't ever wanna see someone on the team in that way, shape or form, so we were really happy he had a clean bill of health, when we left there."

"It had been a Season when Jael had been on the road, so I had never been there for the first investigation," Ryder shared. "Romania is an incredible place, and I think that entire place has this old feeling to it, then you walk into this forest and you're kind of transported back in time. It's very, very bizarre."

FUNNY CREW QUOTE: **Ryder**: "Protect me, oh Lord, from all the [expletive] that Josh Gates gets me into. Why do I do this?" - **Season 5, Episode 6**

"What is life like after *Destination Truth*? Boring, really, I would say," Rex told fans on *DT Fan Radio*. "No, I'm keeping busy. Of course, it's not as exciting as, you know, traveling the world and being part of these awesome investigations, obviously, that goes without saying."

Rex at the time of the interview was working on an RN medical program and aimed to be able to work in pediatrics, critical care, or in an ICU. Ironically enough, he did not return for more *DT* filming so that he could complete this RN program, but he just hopped right back into the world of producing and working for further television programs.

"Josh at this point is one of my best friends," Evan said in our interview. "Think of it. A best friend is someone who you have life experiences with, almost die with and party with." Evan said we can look forward to many more Josh and Evan adventures on *Expedition Unknown* in the future, as Season 3 of the show is filming as this very book is being written.

"Best job of my life, hands down," Evan said of *DT*. "Talk about an adventure. We are seven people doing a TV show in less than favorable conditions. Oh, the stories…That job was the base for my future career as an adventure filmmaker."

CHAPTER 5:
SEASON THREE

When we came back from the mid-season finale during Season Two, we saw that there was quite a change in vibe to *DT*. With the arrival of Season Three, we saw lots more changes come up.

One of the biggest shifts right off the bat was with the show's intro animation. The animation is the logo sitting on a hilltop with the sun setting behind it in a pink-blue twilight color and the sky fades to a twilight blue tone. Along with big sponsorships, cameos from other Syfy program personalities, and many other firsts, the third season took us on a wild ride.

One of Season Three's celebrity guest investigators Allison Scagliotti (AKA "Scags") of *Warehouse 13* sat down with the fan site and spoke of her experience being on the show. She said "my least favorite part would have been sitting in the cemetery in the dark by myself for half an hour. That was terrifying. My favorite part was dancing in the street with everyone! That was so much fun - we were drenched and dehydrated afterwards, but it was a blast...I'd love to go back on the show, preferably if they went to Tahiti."

Another Season Three guest was Dustin Pari of *Ghost Hunters* and *Ghost Hunters International*. In an interview with the fan site, he told us "It was a really good time. I really enjoyed working with Josh, Jael, Rex, and the whole crew. I stay in touch with them all here and there. We were down in Peru and I actually ended up really sick afterwards. They made pasta and I was like 'this seems like a safe dish!' I didn't realize they cook it in water from the river, which is not a good idea, so I ended up really sick, but it was a lot of fun! I got stuck in quick sand, I got bit by some random spider. Not as safe as doing ghost hunting, but it was a lot of fun."

Season 3, Episode 1
Destinations: Romania & the Yucatán
Cases: Hoia Baciu Forest & the Alux
Original Air Date: September 9th, 2009

An immense forest located in Romania is famed for anomalous lights, terrifying specters and a perfectly circular grove in which no vegetation will grow. Josh and a fresh new crew embark on a trek to the Hoia Baciu forest, which would become one of the most notorious and haunting of all *DT* investigations.

Similar to Iceland Elves and Brownies of Celtic lore, the Alux in the second half of this episode are said to be small, trickster imps. Prevalent in the Yucatan regions of Mexico, these diminutive sprites can be a boon or a scourge, depending on how they are treated. Locals often build small dwellings for them in roadside nooks to ensure the Alux are pacified.

Team *DT* sets off to investigate this Mexican mystery. After a memorable night in the Yucatan nightlife, they embark into the dark caves of the region, with intriguing archaeological evidence uncovered.

"The Haunted Forest was a real game changer for me," **Evan B. Stone said in an email interview with the fan site from Spring of 2016 about the first half of this memorable episode**. "At that point, I have never been on camera, so this was my first time for *DT*, and man it did not disappoint. That night, I felt violated and scared. I still have those wounds on my arm. They are permanent - a constant reminder of that night."

"What the camera did not see was the last thing I remember before blacking out," **Evan continued in the interview.** "I was being dragged somehow. As far as recuperating, I had Zero of that. Our next stop in the show was a few days away, which was Chernobyl, and there was no time to waste. I don't tell many people what happened that night, for there was more that happened. Maybe in the next interview!"

Josh VO: "Though he's a ringer for Gene Shallot, Professor Adrian Patrut is actually Romania's leading expert on the Hoia Bochu forest." **Professor**: "There are also sometimes biological effects. States of nausea, of headache, of anxiety. Vomiting." **Josh**: "Sounds like my prom night."

Josh: "This guy just told all these people that I'm in the Batman movie! I'm never leaving Merida. Ever!"

Season 3, Episode 2
Destinations: Mexico & the Bahamas
Cases: Doll Island & the Lusca
Original Air Date: September 16th, 2009

Sufferers of pediophobia may want to skip this expedition. On a small island outside the capital of Mexico, there exists a legend of a drowned girl and her caretaker. The caretaker has adorned the island with dozens of dolls to appease the girl's restless spirit, and these creepy dolls may be supernaturally charged today. With this information in hand, Josh, Jael and the crew embark on a harrowing, haunting journey to La Isla de la Muñecas AKA the Island of the Dolls.

Next, Captain Nemo, or Jack Sparrow for a more contemporary example, are famous for their tangles with giant cephalopods. On Andros Island in the Bahamas, there is tale of a true-to-life massive octopus beast known as the Lusca. With tentacles said to stretch beyond 80 feet, the creature is a legitimate leviathan. Utilizing cavernous aquatic entry points known as "blue holes", Josh dives deep into the briny depths.

Josh: "We got a real *Brokeback Mountain* vibe going on here. Mike, I wish I knew how to quit you!"

Josh: "If that doll opens its eye, I will [expletive] in my pants."

Josh: "How drunk is too drunk to run a hardware store?"

Season 3, Episode 3
Destinations: Egypt & Florida (USA)
Cases: King Tut's Tomb & Skunk Ape
Original Air Date: September 23rd, 2008

Tutankhamen was a boy who spent the entirety of his teenage years, and the remainder of his young life, as Pharaoh of the 18th dynasty of Egypt. Although he was but a minor ruler in the dynastic timeline, his legacy became world famous to the 20th century during the 1923 uncovering of his tomb by Howard Carter. Perhaps more infamous than the treasures found within, there is an alleged deadly curse said to afflict many of the archaeological expeditions that disturbed his rest.

Attaining special permission from the Egyptian government, Team Truth ventures into the Valley of the Kings. There, they delve into the mysterious famous tomb and encounter strange voices and shadows within.

If Sasquatch is synonymous with the Northwestern U.S., then the Skunk Ape holds claim to the Southeast. The beast is said to be a large hominid possessing a distinctly nasty smell and makes its habitat in the Everglades of Florida.

Team *DT* embarks on a fan boat driven expedition in this, their very first investigation on American soil. Encounters with local wildlife and unusual heat signatures lead the team to question what exactly is making a big stink in the Everglades.

Josh VO: "Growing up a Boston baseball fan, I know a thing or two about curses."

Josh VO: "A stinky, hairy ape man is stalking the swamps of Florida, and it's not a frat boy or a great-grandpa gone wild."

Season 3, Episode 4
Destinations: The Ukrane & Egypt
Cases: Haunted Chernobyl & the Sal'Awa
Original Air Date: September 30th, 2009

On April 26, 1986 a power surge in a nuclear reactor in the Ukranian town of Pripyat caused an explosion. The result was a plume of radioactive fallout that would forever taint the surrounding region. Biological effects plague the region to this day and now, alleged paranormal activity can be added to the list.

Josh and the team don precautionary information from local experts and protective gear to investigate the haunted halls of the abandoned, irradiated commune. With radiation leaks spiking and nerves fraying, will the team suffer a mental fallout, or will they uncover the secrets hidden in the shadows of Chernobyl?

The Sal'Awa (arabic for "Scary Dog") is a canine cryptid that is said to haunt the cane fields of rural Egypt, preying on all who cross its path. This expedition takes the team from the sands of the desert to the rural regions of Cairo. What kind of canine creature stalks the fields, emitting menacing growls in the dark of night? Is it merely a local feral dog, or something much more mysterious?

Josh VO: "A disaster of a different scale awaited us at baggage claim. the Ukranian airways baggage handlers appear to still be fighting the Cold War against our luggage, and winning." **Josh**: "It's like a pack of wild gorillas are working in baggage handling."

Josh: "On the list of dining destinations world wide that I always thought I would take a pass on, the Chernobyl cafeteria might be at the top of that list…It's not like microwaved food. It's like eating inside the microwave."

Josh: "Okay, I kissed the cobra, I kissed the cobra. I also just peed my pants."

Season 3, Episode 5
Destinations: Chile & Turkey
Cases: Chile UFOs & Lake Van Monster
Original Air Date: October 7th, 2009

UFOlogist Josef Hynek established the classic scale for rating alleged encounters with extraterrestrials. Thanks to Spielberg's seminal film *Close Encounters of The Third Kind*, the public is most familiar with what is construed as actual contact with an alien being.

Things may be getting a bit too close in Northern Chile, as tales have emerged of mummified bodies of small, humanoid creatures being found. In conjunction with mysterious lights in the sky, some claim these bodies to be the remains of extraterrestrials. The destination for our crew is a deserted mine as they rappel into a vertical shaft to look for these remains.

Lake Van lies in Eastern Turkey, which is a large body of water said to harbor a monstrous secret. "Van Golu Canavari" is said to be a large prehistoric throwback creature that is almost certainly a carnivore. A video supposedly depicting the aquatic beast spurs the team into action. Cold, dark, wet adventure awaits as the crew scours the depths of the Middle Eastern lake in their search for the truth.

Josh VO: "After touching down, we grabbed our gear and headed to the rental car counter, where we adventurers don't tend to be too popular."
Josh: "I will need full insurance coverage." **Clerk**: "Si." **Josh**: "Because I'm gonna flip it." **Clerk**: "Heh."

Josh: "Where do they even get these cars from? Where?! Oh, look at this - it comes with a filthy pillow. With a pair of underwear under it. 'Oh, Josh Gates is coming to town. Give him the car from *Green Acres*."

Season 3, Episode 6
Destinations: Peru & the Bermuda Islands
Cases: Chullachaqui & the Bermuda Triangle
Original Air Date: October 14th, 2009

The South American country of Peru plays host to a great menagerie of diverse creatures and allegedly, a small trickster sprite. The Chullachaqui is essentially the South American leprechaun, being a small creature that can bring luck or misery to whomever it encounters. The small spirit's most distinguishing feature is it's unusual backwards pointing feet.

The jungles of Peru is where Team Truth, along with Dustin and Robb of *Ghost Hunters International,* brave the perils of the wilderness in search of the truth. Will the snakes and quicksand bury the truth, or will they uncover clues to this tiny terror?

The Bermuda Triangle is the next case - a legend amongst strange phenomena, stretching roughly 1 million miles between the three points off the coast of Florida, Puerto Rico and the Bermuda Islands. This stretch of open ocean has been responsible for mysterious, recorded disappearances since the 1950's.

Josh and the team embark on a triple threat investigation of land, sea and air. Utilizing the Bahamian island of Bimini as base camp, will they be the latest to succumb to the mysteries of the triangle and vanish within?

Josh: "Dustin, as a thank you for being on *DT*, compliments of the show, you're getting a full blown case of malaria." **Dustin Pari**: "Sweet, thanks." **Josh**: "That's the gift that keeps on giving!"

Josh: "How do we drive here - left side or right side? **Bicha**: "We're doing left." **Josh**: "I want to know what the island is doing, though." **Bicha**: "Right. I'm sorry, left." **Josh**: "This might be a quick episode."

Season 3, Episode 7
Destinations: Peru & Alaska USA
Cases: Haunted Lost City & the Thunderbird
Original Air Date: October 21st, 2009

Tucked away in Peru, in the shadow of the Andes Mountains and Machu

Pichu, there exists an abandoned city with a dark reputation. Local farmers refuse to cross the mountain impass for fear of the spectral figures sighted amongst the ruins. Our intrepid explorers venture up a steep, treacherous pass to reach their destination. With reports of mysterious, phantom bells fresh in their mind, will the team experience for whom the bells toll, deep in the Peruvian night?

The next case is the Thunderbird, with stories of this massive avian cryptid (aka The Roc) dating centuries back amongst the natives of the most frontier of North America. More modern tales range from a missing alleged photograph from the old Arizona west to the infamous Lawndale incident. In this particular account, a small child in 1977 from Illinois was actually picked up and carried several feet by a similar large bird!

Josh and the team travel to the Alaskan village of Manokotak for a chilly expedition. They take a snowmobile-led journey into the night, scanning the skies for the winged wonder. What mysteries soar above the Alaskan tundra? Team Truth is determined to find out.

Josh: "People say 'Josh, what's the most dangerous thing you've ever done on *DT*?' I'll tell you right now - it's showering in here. I'm supposed to grip this metal handle while soaking wet, which is wired to a bare light bulb, and then I am supposed to flip that switch. I mean, there is not enough liquor in the universe for me to flip that switch."

Josh: "It's foggy and a little late in the day, but I'm pretty sure there's a unicorn behind me."

Josh: "That guy has a dead animal on his head! It's not even a hat - he just killed an animal and strapped it to his head."

Season 3, Episode 8
Destinations: Romania & Chile
Cases: Romania Werewolf & Chilean Dinosaurs
Original Air Date: October 28th, 2009

We've already encountered lupine legends in South America. Now, it's time to head back to the old country as Team Truth heads to Vlad Dracul's homeland, Romania. Barring any *Underworld* style fisticuffs, the village of Brad is supposedly being menaced by a flesh and blood werewolf. Armed with a fresh bottle of "werewolf wine" and raw meat, the crew embarks on a dark hunt into the Romanian wilderness to seek out the hairy howler.

The second case finds us back into the realm of living dinosaurs. Seemingly every subgroup of dinos have been sighted in the Atacama desert of Northern Chile, and there is said to lurk a velociraptor-type beast. The creature has been sighted keeping pace with cars on the highway and is said to sport a distinctive three-toed track.

Josh and team embark on a treacherous desert hunt, seeking a water source that might lead to a creature population. There, amidst a haunting desert cemetery, they discover potential evidence for the Cretaceous creeper.

Josh: "Werewolf wine. And there are descriptions on how to spot a werewolf on the back of here. This is not booze - this is an investigation tool!"

Josh: "Some people said I would never find a dinosaur in Chile. They were wrong. Also, I found an old photo of Joan Crawford, so that's two dinosaurs."

Season 3, Episode 9
Destination: Bhutan
Case: Yeti
Original Air Date: November 4th, 2009

In a rare continuation expedition, Josh and the team tackle the legend of the Yeti yet again. Our intrepid explorers set off for the Bhutan wilderness, encountering unique local customs and plenty of things going bump in the night. Hiking further and further into the wilderness, they scour canyons, forests and caves in this new trek for the team's most elusive yet promising journey.

Josh: "Sightings of Bigfoot and his descendants are reported around the world as often as I Google my own name."

Josh: "Did that Monk's cell phone just go off?!" **Josh VO**: "Even here in the last refuge against the modern world, free nights and weekends are still a big draw."

Season 3, Episode 10
Destinations: Israel & Ireland
Cases: Haunted Masada & Leprechauns
Original Air Date: March 17th, 2010

Masada is an ancient construct in Israel with ties to the Biblical figure of King Herod. It has a turbulent past, withstanding the assault of Roman forces in a massive war between the Romans and Jewish forces, which ended in a tragic mass suicide. The ruins of this fortress rest on a giant plateau overlooking the Dead Sea. While said body of water is infamous for hosting little to no life, its massive neighbor might play host to scores of disturbed residents of the afterlife. Team Truth investigates reports of phantom drums and strange voices.

Then, the Leprechaun is one of the most culturally well-known legends on Josh's investigation itinerary. Whether it be menacing Jennifer Aniston in a cheesy slasher film or keeping his breakfast cereal from greedy children, the spritely Irish prankster is a trans-continental phenomenon. However, Ireland plays host to the true legend, forgoing the bright green, clover obsessed stereotype and presenting a classic Celtic figure bedecked in red garb.

The notorious Leprechaun has extensive tales surrounding it, amongst the most well known being his coveted pot of gold and his penchant for trickery. The *DT* crew heads to the Emerald Isle to scour the caves and hillsides for an entrance to the faerie realm. Will Irish eyes smile on the team as they hunt for these elusive, tricky imps?

Josh: "Hi, I'm gonna need a new rental car. I'm the guy in the big, yellow [expletive]-box, you can't miss me. As soon as you can. Shalom!"

Josh VO: "This truly is a mecca for sacred t-shirts, wholesale menorahs, and divine table wear." **Josh**: "They have some Last Supper placemats which nothing says 'classy' like putting a bowl of spaghetti on top of Jesus."

Josh VO: "I was disappointed we couldn't take a sample, so I did what was natural, and drowned my sorrows over a pint with my crew."

Season 3, Episode 11
Destinations: China & Israel
Cases: Haunted Great Wall & Mermaid
Original Air Date: March 24th, 2010

The Great Wall. The first incarnation of this world famous architectural landmark was constructed in BC times by the first emperor of China, Qin Shi Huang. The main wall itself stretches about 4000 miles with at least another 1500 miles consisting of natural extensions of the border.

Naturally, an architectural feat on such a massive scale, which is visible from space, was very labor intensive. It is the spirits of these workers and the soldiers that are said to stalk the stone confines of the wall.

For this unique investigation, Team Truth is granted permission by the Chinese government to scour a portion of the wall that has been reclaimed by nature. The team investigates and encounters very interesting evidence as they explore for signs of the paranormal.

In *DT* lore, mermaids are known for being one of the two creatures investigated in the very first televised episode. Josh and the team are now hot on the trail for a different finned wonder that has been sighted in the waves off the coast of Kiryat Yam, Israel.

The humanoid creature has a $1 Million bounty for it's capture but Team Truth is in it purely for scientific purposes. Well, MAINLY scientific purposes. The team embarks on a two-phase hunt, with a daylight caving expedition and a moonlit dive into the depths of sunken ruins.

Josh: "A black backpack. Swiffer. World War II fuel container. Bottle of moonshine. And a tiny fire extinguisher. Ryder, did you pack this car?" **Ryder**: "Yes!"

Josh: "That scared the [expletive] out of me. Crazy Chinese ghosts."

Season 3, Episode 12
Destinations: New Jersey USA & China
Cases: The Jersey Devil & the Yeren

The Jersey Devil is Americana myth personified. Featured in countless movies, shows, video games and even the namesake of a NHL hockey team, the beast is true legend. The chimeric creature is said to resemble a kangaroo, a bat, a deer, or all of the above! It holds folkloric origins that say the monstrosity is actually the 13th child of a witch named Mother Leeds, who conceived this child with the Devil himself.

Kris Williams of the *Ghost Hunters International* team joins us on a rare USA *DT* investigation. They search both the skies and the forest trails of the New Jersey Pine Barrens in the hunt for America's ultimate camp fire legend.

Next, the Yeren or "Wildman of China," is essentially the Far East's cousin to that North-Western American staple, Sasquatch. Sightings of the hairy hominid run rampant in Eastern China. The beast has even been popularized in Western culture for tangling with Kurt Russell in *Big Trouble in Little China*.

Shennongjia Park in Eastern Hubei Province is the venue for this next expedition. Josh invites Jael de Pardo back into the fold as they trek deep into the wilderness. They encounter treacherous bridges and motion sensor alarms in their quest for China's resident mystery primate.

Josh: "Every country in the world? Free luggage carts. America? 4 dollars for one luggage cart!" **Mike**: "Ice cream used to cost a quarter!" **Josh**: "What, are you sixty [years old]?!"

Josh: "Last time I saw you was-" **Kris**: "Prison." **Josh**: "Was in prison. Our night at the Essex County Penitentiary." **Kris**: "I don't know why they let us out."

Josh: "Let's get out of this town before we get arrested."

Josh: "This is a pretty substantial pile of [expletive]." **Mike**: "That is a monster deuce, man!"

Season 3, Episode 13
Destinations: Chile & New Zealand
Cases: Haunted Mining Towns & Taniwha
Original Air Date: April 7th, 2010

La Noria and Humberstone are two notorious mining towns located in Northern Chile. Both towns have long been shut down, with pasts of neglect and barbaric treatment of its inhabitants. It is this negative energy that has stained the area with dark shadows of the unsettled dead.

This expedition begins with a recon paragliding mission and becomes a wholly unique adventure. Actress Allison Scagliotti joins the team in what becomes a hybrid archeological/paranormal investigation.

La Noria plays host to actual human remains and an unsettling isolation session for Ryder. Humberstone sees the team venture indoors to the abandoned buildings for more paranormal sweeps. Two abandoned towns to be scoured, but how populated will they be with the restless souls of the departed?

The Taniwha ("Tah-nee-fah") are a new entry into the *DT* pantheon as we explore Maori culture for the first time. To the indigenous people of New Zealand, the Taniwha are portrayed variously as protective guardians and predatory monsters. Appropriately, their physical appearance is also disputed, having been described as fish-like or more like a serpentine eel. One standard remains, in that they are reportedly haunting the waters of inland Oceania.

Josh visits the Rotorua region of New Zealand and immerses himself in the local Maori culture. He and the team dive into the local lakes, braving cold water and noxious swarms of insects. Will the legends of the Taniwha prove benevolent, or does the team have more to fear in the New Zealand waters?

Josh: "Can I ask you a question? Why are you wearing a totally see-through shirt? **Evan**: "It's silk." **Josh**: "There's a lot of nipple happening right now." **Ryder**: "Somebody get Evan a coat, please!"

Josh VO: "We passed through a sprawling local market where the sea food was fresh, and uncooked." **Josh**: "You want some raw fish? In this heat, it really takes the edge off, Gabe." **Josh VO**: "Scags (Allison) got a real taste of *DT* fine dining." **Josh**: "It's a giant bucket of raw fish guts and it's delicious. Are you gonna be sick right here?" **Allison**: "Uh huh." **Josh**: "Don't puke on camera. That's rule number 7." **Allison**: "I didn't get the rule book!"

Season 3, Episode 14
Destinations: Jordan & South Carolina USA
Cases: Ghosts of Petra & the Lizard Man
Original Air Date: April 14th, 2010

The team heads back to the Middle East to explore an ancient Jordanian city called Petra. This is no ordinary ghost hunt, as the ruins are said to be populated by the Djinn.

These ancient Arabian spirits are known in Western popular culture as Genies. Forget *Aladdin*'s most popular character, Jambi from *Pee Wee's Playhouse*, or *Kazaam* (you'll seriously want to forget this one), these spirits are more known as theological, mystical figures rather than the granter of wishes. They hold a heavy presence in the Quran and are known to have either a benevolent or destructive nature.

Team Truth wanders amongst the abandoned buildings and majestic amphitheaters of this once proud settlement. Will their wish for evidence be granted, or will they find themselves stranded in the Jordanian ruins as they scour the sands of time?

Next, the backwoods of South Carolina are reportedly home to another American legend, although not nearly as old as the Jersey Devil. The 7-foot reptilian humanoid know as the Lizard Man was first reported in the late 1980's and has made several sporadic appearances since then.

The citizens of Bishopville regard the creature as a type of cute and popular mascot, despite its predatory behavior. It seems to favor attacking cars, perhaps viewing terrified motorists as canned food! Josh and team find surprising evidence in the quest to see if the creature still has bite as they explore the marshland of the Scape Ore Swamp.

Josh: "Vanessa doesn't have her bag?" **Ryder**: "Still not yet. Her baggage hasn't shown up yet. She's wearing your underwear, not mine." **Josh**: "She could wear my underwear as a pair of pants!"

Ryder: "Green beans, green beans, get 'em while they're hot!"

Ryder: "This one can be your Flavor Flav Djinn medallion." **Josh**: "Yeah! Could you knock, like, ten of my teeth out?" **Ryder**: It would be my honor."

Josh VO: "I treated myself to a local Lizard Man makeover." **Josh**: "Will this fit me?" **Local Shop Clerk**: "It was made for a smaller person." **Josh**: "Sir, are you saying I'm fat?!"

Located in the South Pacific, 1200 miles off the coast of Chile, Easter Island is an incredibly enigmatic piece of land. It boasts a population of about 6000, not counting the near 900 famous Moai statues that dot the coast. These intriguing stone busts were crafted by the Rapa Nui tribes and are said to represent the spirits of their ancestors. According to local residents, this may be taken in the literal sense, as these monolithic statues are supposedly haunted.

After imbibing in local ceremonial tea, the team sets up camp at the Tongariki altar on the Southern tip of the island. Until Season 5, this will be Team Truth's most remote investigation, considerably amping the danger factor, alongside some paranormal happenings.

Then, it's back to Kiwi Country as our intrepid explorers set off to scour the glacial region of New Zealand for a population of giant bird called the Moa. This big bird, driven to extinction by local tribes, was most closely related to the modern cassowary and emu, said to stand at a massive 10 to 12 feet tall. Much like other supposedly extinct creatures like the Dodo or Thylacine, or of course, that old standard of the living dinosaur, reports are collected of living populations of this most ardent of avians.

Team Truth sets off on top of the glacial region of the island and into the dense forests on their expedition. The group finds interesting evidence, supplying more pieces of the puzzle in the hunt for this huge, wingless wonder.

Josh VO: "A place we could only find if I could get the GPS to stop yelling at me in Chinese." **Josh**: "It speaks everything but English! I think it just swore at me! I think, I did, I just ordered a burrito on this thing. That's like a

Star Wars language. What?! It's like the *It's a Small World* of GPS units."

Ryder: "Evan, what's going on?" **Josh**: What the [expletive] is wrong with you?!" **Evan**: "[expletive] ants all over me!" **Josh**: "There's nothing on you!" **Evan**: "You sure?" **Josh**: "Look at you! You're like a maniac!"

SEASON THREE MILESTONES:
- **S3 (general)** - *Orbitz.com* sponsorship. *Destination Truth* also had a commercial that advertised *Nationwide Insurance*, in which Josh narrated it and proclaimed the insurance company's slogan, set to dramatic music and scenes from the show
- **S3 E1** - First cameo by cast members of another Syfy show appear
- **S3 E3** - First overnight paranormal investigation in Tut's tomb EVER & first American investigation on the show (second half of episode)
- **S3 E4** - First overnight Chernobyl paranormal investigation EVER
- **S3 E5** - First alien investigation on the show
- **S3 E6** - Guest investigators (not evidence reviewers) Robb Demarest and Dustin Pari of *Ghost Hunters International*
- **S3 E10** - First overnight paranormal investigation of Masada EVER
- **S3 E12** - Kris Williams of *Ghost Hunters* and *Ghost Hunters International* investigates with the crew
- **S3 E13** - Allison Scagliotti of *Warehouse 13* is a guest investigator
- **S3 E14** - First overnight investigation of Petra EVER

CHAPTER 6:
FAN QUESTIONS & EVIDENCE

You remember the feeling. The humor, travel and suspense of each episode. Then, we got to the juicy stuff - the evidence review. This section is dedicated to listing the experts who reviewed evidence on the show, but not before we get some answers to popular fan questions you likely have had over the years about evidence, the cast, or even just the show itself.

WHY DID WE ONLY GET ONE SEASON OF *DT* ON DVD? The basic answer is that it was NBC/Universal and Syfy's decision. Josh spoke about this on *DT Fan Radio*: "The DVD thing is without a doubt the single most asked question for *Destination Truth*. I get emails about it, people Twitter about it...I just have no information about that. You know, I know that for *Ghost Hunters*, actually a third party got involved to release the DVD's. They weren't released by the channel. What I can say is that *DT* is on iTunes...I wish I had some DVD info for you, and I don't. I think in the mean time, iTunes is probably the way to go." **Why didn't *DT* use a third party to release DVDs?** We were never given an answer to that, but since *Ghost Hunters* was a more popular show, and is even still on the air with new episodes on Syfy to this day, they likely had a bigger budget to work with and felt it would be good for the TAPS (The Atlantic Paranormal Society) brand to release their own DVDs, but again, this is just a theory.

● **WHY WERE FANS NEVER ON THE SHOW? Though it technically never happened (except for a surprising fact revealed ahead), Josh and Ping Pong Productions tried many times. On a *DT Fan Radio* episode, Josh said:** "We have talked about at length actually, ways in which we can involve viewers and fans of the show, on the show. We've certainly talked about everything from, you know, contests, to inviting people to participate, to format changes where things like that would happen and the reality is, is that it's a long conversation that we have with the channel, that we have with ourselves and I think we'd like nothing more than to be able to go out into the field with some folks who've never been out there before."

Josh continued "You know, our medic on the show this year Rex, who you see in the episodes, he is a guy who was a real fan of the show and had not been extensively well-traveled before we hired him to join us this season. Being able to be out there with him and see his experiences...someone who'd watched the show, and was now getting the chance to not only travel to these places, but to see how the show was made, was a really fun experience for us. We'd love to do more of that and find ways to bring new folks onto the show."

● **WHY DID THE CREW CHANGE SO MUCH? Josh spoke about this on *DT Fan Radio*, saying**: "It's sort of a question we get a lot, actually, is why the crew kind of rotates around. The reality of reality television is that a lot of production jobs - camera operators and audio technicians, other positions - they're very catch-as-catch-can. So because we have kind of an erratic filming schedule, we'll come home and stay home to work on the edited post for a few months. Then, these guys just take other jobs and are unavailable. We've had shooters on our show that have gone and done *Amazing Race*, *Survivor*, *Top Chef*, and we had the case this Season (Season 3) where we had some people who were simply unavailable for the rotation."

● **WHY DIDN'T THE CREW SPEND MORE TIME AT EACH LOCATION FOR THE INVESTIGATIONS? Josh told us:** "One of the criticisms we get a lot on the show is, like, why don't you spend more time at each location? And believe me, we feel the same way. We wish we could spend a week doing overnight investigations looking for these creatures, but unfortunately, the production schedule dictates a certain time table, and I guess our feeling in the end is that it's better to spend a few nights than none at all. So, in some places, we will film, if it's a story let's say closer to civilization as it were, it could be as few as four days. And we went to Bhutan in an episode that will be airing later this season that was about a 12-day expedition, so it really depends on the story and how hard it is to get to the story."

● **WHY DIDN'T THEY EVER CATCH ANYTHING THEY WERE AFTER ON THE SHOW? A surprising evaluation from Josh taught us:** "At the end of the day, that's an important thing that people have to realize is that we are trying to do something that is illuminating on some sort of an academic level, that we are showing people cultures they have never seen before. We're talking about important stories in folklore, but at the same time, if nobody tunes in and watches it because it's just me talking for an hour about the history of a certain civilization, then we don't have a show to put on the air…it's not easy to throw a net over an animal if you're there for a few nights, but I think it's better to go and even if in some cases, it's scratching the surface, it's certainly bringing these interesting stories to our viewers and letting them see places they've never seen before. We hope that excites people and encourages them to go and invest in these stories and in these cultures and you know, that hopefully keeps the search going."

● **WAS ANY OF THE EVIDENCE ON *DT* EVER FAKED? Josh tells us:** "We have a real mandate from ourselves and from the Syfy channel to be legitimate. We want to go out there, really get our hands dirty and set up a credible investigation for whatever we're looking for. But we're also cognitive of the fact that we are making a show to entertain people, and so it's always important that we, you know, present something that isn't strictly cut and dry field work. There has to be some excitement to it."

Josh spoke further on an important criticism of *DT*, saying "Some people say 'Well, how come you got a person on the team who gets scared or runs away, or does this and does that?' Fundamentally, all those things kind of add to the flavor of the show. But when it comes to the things that we find or the experiences we're having out there, all of that is 'what you see is what you get,' because we're certainly not going to fabricate any of the evidence that we collect on the show…a lot of the things that we find end up being hair fibers from known animals or evidence of things that, at the end of the day, we do have an answer for. Certainly, I think that if we wanted to fabricate things, I'd be out there in an animatronic Bigfoot suit."

● **WHY DIDN'T *DT* EVER DO A PARANORMAL CASE CENTERED ON THE CONCENTRATION CAMPS FROM NAZI GERMANY? Josh spoke of this at a San Diego Comic Con press room, telling the fan**

site: "We talked about doing a sort of Nazi-related thing, and I think we all felt like it was too difficult. it's just too sensitive and I don't think anyone had the comfort level that they wanted to do it. We felt like, beyond the fact that it just had a certain sensitivity involved with it, it just, you know, I actually never had an opportunity to visit any of the World War II camps, but everyone I talked to who spent time there says it's just so impacting and difficult. I think that's something we just have always felt would be best to just step clear of."

WHO DID THE WRITING AND ART ON THE *DT* OFFICE CHALKBOARDS? Josh revealed: "My handwriting is terrible. It's not always the same person. Ryder has written a lot of the boards, Jael has written some of the boards, and other people in the room who have neat handwriting have contributed to them, but it's not always the same person."

LIKELY THE MOST-ASKED FAN QUESTION - DID THE CREW EVER FIND OUT WHAT THAT CARCASS WAS THAT THEY FOUND UNDERGROUND (from S3 E5)? In terms of the "alien mummy" looking thing found during this investigation, Josh revealed on *DT Fan Radio*: "That's a heartbreaker in some ways, because that corpse, and that's what it is, it's a corpse. I mean it stank to high hell, it was in a state of decomposition. Rex, who's a paramedic, took a good look at it. He basically felt on site that it wasn't a bird, even though it sorta looked like a chicken in some ways but we felt like it was not. We felt like it was not human - certainly, the anatomy looked wrong for it to be human, and we couldn't bring it back here and put it on a lab table. You just can't transport like something, you know, something like that legally. And so we photographed it, sampled it to death and left it with local authorities. We're still in contact with them and trying to get an answer on what their findings are. In the meantime, we were sort of amazed that we stumped our experts here, but at the same time, a little discouraged because then we really wish we had the actual sample back with us again." Ever since that interview, we still haven't received any further information from local authorities in Chile, so this will likely forever remain a mystery.

WHY WERE THERE SO LITTLE CASES/EPISODES SHOT IN AMERICA? **Josh told us:** "There was a concern that we didn't want the show to lose what everybody at the channel and our offices felt like was really part of the success of the show, is this really exotic flavor that it has. And that we take viewers to places that are really off the beaten path. So our initial fear was that we would jeopardize that by shooting in the US, but both of the episodes that we did this season in the US are really remote and really difficult. The outer frontier of Alaska is as hard a place that we've probably ever shot in. So I think that people will, we hope, watch those episodes and realize that there's a lot of adventure right in their own backyard."

WHAT HAPPENED WITH *DESTINATION DINNERS*? No idea. That's a question for Josh that has since to be answered in the past few years, but I'm assuming that since he announced it in 2012, the same year that *DT* later fell into limbo, that may have had something to do with it. This was a concept Josh came up with and announced at a convention called C2E2 in 2012 a little while before Season 5 aired - the idea was that he would post a location somewhere in the world where he would pay for a communal dinner amongst himself and fans, then take them on a local tour of the location, and that he would even use his many frequent flier miles to pay for one lucky fan's trip to get to the location and back. Since Josh could have been waiting for the status of when the show was coming back before committing to such trips, plus dealing with his own personal life, it likely was a good idea that fell to the wayside. He also just had a child, within less than a year of this book being published, but I'm sure since his frequent flier miles keep growing, he can always do this in the future!

SINCE IT WAS MET WITH MIXED REVIEWS AND WAS FORMALLY CANCELED (UNLIKE *DT*), WHAT DID JOSH REALLY THINK OF HIS SIDE PROJECT *STRANDED*? He said: "I have to say, any and all promotional bull[expletive], I'm really proud of the show…I've had an amazing last five years shooting *DT*, and that really is my passion, is to be working in travel. That's what I love to do, but to be able to work with Brad and Casey at Ping Pong Productions and to work with Jason Blum on a totally new type of show is really satisfying. I really had a great time."

WHY DID *DESTINATION TRUTH* END? The answer sadly is that we likely will never know. Like the stories of ghosts and creatures passed down from generation to generation around the world, we can only guess and do our own research on the topic. I will present you with the evidence we have. Not conspiracy theories, but basic evidence.

Mostly, we can deduct that it is business related, as Josh stated in his 2014 public notice "having reached the end of my second consecutive deal with NBC Universal, we decided that this was the right time to bring the series to a close." Since I see many fans asking me as a fan site runner (thinking I'm Josh) and Josh himself to "bring the show back," they hopefully see it wasn't his show, but rather that it belonged to a network.

Anyhow, Josh's answer is understandable, but **why did we go two years with nothing?** Josh even confirmed and apologized for having to be quiet about it for a while, despite, as he said, "thousands of emails, tweets, letters, mildly creepy packages, and the occasional shout from passing cars asking me about the future of *Destination Truth*."

Many *DT* fans were likely familiar with how the show was shot and then aired. We would get a half of a season, then a hiatus for them to film more, then the other half would air on TV months after. We got seven episodes of season 5 that aired between July and August of 2012. We then (not so patiently) waited to hear from the crew, from Josh, or Syfy when Team Truth was going to go back on the road to film the back half of Season 5.

Perhaps some extra help to us is this quote I got in an interview with Saul Rubinek of *Warehouse 13*, another Syfy program, on a possible issue regarding viewer counts: "I can tell you one thing - I think that even though we are the Number One show and have been for three years in Syfy's history, I think they're underestimating how many people are watching our show and I can tell you why. I have a daughter in college. You know how many people in college watch television sets? None! They're watching that (points to a smart phone), they're watching [on] their computers. So when they see it on the internet, this show, they're getting advertising, aren't they? Yes, they are. Can they turn off the advertising? No, they can't. So, why aren't we being counted?"

Saul continued in the interview, saying "I had a long period, because I'm very old, I have people recognizing me from *Frasier*, *True Romance*, *Unforgiven*, and I can tell usually, 'you know, man, that guy's got tattoos - he likes *True Romance*, I can tell' but this show, they're all ages. All walks of life…they're underestimating by half how many people are actually watching the show…it's not counted properly."

JOSH SAYS:

"At the end of the day, we really live and die by the viewership of the show."

During this silence from 2012 to 2014, it was confusing to us, since Syfy appeared to still be making use of both Josh Gates and Ping Pong Productions. We were treated to a project Josh directly participated in producing for Syfy called "Stranded," which aired for a few months in the first half of 2013, but in September of 2014, it was canceled. Josh was even in a Syfy clip show called *Insane or Inspired?* the same year as Season 5. He was also part of the Syfy 20th Anniversary special in December 2012, cameo'ed in a *Ghost Hunters* episode in November 2012, as well as another *GH* episode in January of 2013. Even Ryder had her own side project in which she was a featured host called *Chasing UFOs* on another network in 2012, but she confirmed to fans in January of 2013 that this was canceled.

Josh also proposed to Hallie in 2013, who was then his girlfriend, and since they were married a few months after we were told *DT* was canceled, we can't say them starting their life together is the reason *DT* ended and it would certainly be a ridiculous, rude theory to even think about. **A celebrity or public figure owes a lot to their fans, but not the total sacrifice of their personal life.** I'm glad the fans love and accept Hallie like they do. It takes a tough woman to let Josh do the crazy things he does and to have her share her valuable time with him by being so nice to the fans is something I am grateful of. Plus, *Expedition Unknown* is Josh's current TV project and has equally dangerous scenarios, so it's safe to say his personal life has nothing to do with it.

Even on my end, as the author of this book and the fan site runner since 2008, I did my best to rally the troops. Along with online petitions, I spent much time poking the @Syfy Twitter runner (then Craig Engler, who I met and is a lovely person). I even approached and met Syfy's President Dave Howe at a book signing Josh did in NYC to tell him about how much we loved *DT*. We loved the show, but that is why TV falls under the category of show business, because ultimately, to most people in television, it is purely business. Fans equal dollars, and the more = the better. With Saul's theory in an earlier paragraph, perhaps Syfy thought there weren't as many of us watching as there really were?

Though we didn't get proper closure with how *DT* ended, this statement written by Josh to the fans is certainly good compensation:

"Finally, I want to thank the fans of *Destination Truth*. We never had any billboards or full-page magazine ads. I don't think they ever ran a commercial that didn't only air on Syfy. But still, you found the show and you stayed tuned. To Amanda and the 'Truthies' who supported us from early on and worked tirelessly to spread the word. Thank you.

"*Destination Truth* wasn't designed to be a cutting-edge show. After all, some of the tales we told have been whispered about since time immemorial. But, I think we found a connection with viewers because we tried to celebrate the timeless appeal of mystery. I like to think that *DT* was, at its best, like a good, old-fashioned campfire story – a bit improvised, slightly rough around the edges, and never taking itself too seriously. Though we did work hard to find the truth, our secret mission was really to promote travel and to take the viewer with us along the way. Thanks for coming along season after season."

 EXPERTS

Here is a list, in no particular order,
of the experts and their distinctions, who
reviewed *DT* episode evidence:

- **Dr. Jim Dines**, mammalogist (S3 E1, S3 E5, S3 E5, S3 E8, S3 E9, S3 E10, S3 E12, S4 E4, S4 E7, S4 E8, S4 E10, S4 E13, S5 E2, S5 E3, & S5 E6)
- **Mike Dee**, zoo curator (S1 E4, S1 E6, S2 E5, S2 E10, S2 E11, S2

E13, S3 E3, S3 E4, S3 E6, S3 E7, S4 E3, S4 E5, S4 E11, S4 E12, & S5 E7)
- **Luis Chiappe PHD**, paleontologist (S3 E8)
- **Dr Scott Cooper**, marine biologist (S2 E8, S2 E10, S2 E12, S3 E2, & S3 E5)
- **Ian Recchio**, herpetologist/ecology (S2 E13)
- **Troy Tackett**, paranormal expert (S2 E11 & S2 E12)
- **Dan Mewhinney**, paranormal expert (S2 E2, S2 E9 & S2 E11)
- **Dr. Cecilia Penedo**, geneticist (S2 E7 & S2 E8)
- **Jeff Dwyer PHD**, paranormal expert (S2 E7)
- **Vu Ngoc Thahn**, zoo curator (S2 E4)
- **Dr. Abdul Sheriff**, cultural research institute exec. director (S2 E4)
- **Dr. MJ Hajianpour MD PhD**, geneticist (S2 E3)
- **Carol Kase**, scientist/researcher (S2 E2)
- **Dr. Melba Ketchum**, forensic analysis (S3 E9 & S3 E12)
- **Mike Schaadt**, aquarium director (S3 E11, S3 E13, S4 E2 & S4 E4)
- **Dr. Jeff Meldrum PhD**, primatologist (S1 E4 & S5 E1)
- **Steve Murillo of MUFON LA**, UFO expert (S5 E4)
- **Dr. Lee Kats**, biology professor (S5 E4 & S5 E5)
- **Dr Andrew Engilis PhD**, zoologist (S1 E1, S1 E2 & S1 E3)
- **Steve Buller & Gregg Stutchman**, video/audio forensics (S1 E2, S1 E3, S1 S4 & S1 E5)
- **Molly Maioum**, Thai translator for EVP analysis (S1 E2)
- **Dr. Elizabeth Wictum PhD**, veterinary geneticist (S1 E3)
- **Dr. Roger Whewell**, geologist (S1 E4)
- **Teri Kun**, DNA specialist (S1 E5 & S1 E6)
- **Dr. Tim Hovey PhD**, fisheries biologist (S1 E4 & S1 E5)
- **Steve Gonsalves & Dave Tango of TAPS**, paranormal experts (S3 E2 & S3 E7)
- **Barry Fitzgerald & Kris Williams of TAPS,** paranormal experts (S4 E10 & S4 E12)
- **Jason Hawes & Grant Wilson of TAPS**, paranormal experts (S3 E1, S3 E4, S3 E10, S3 E11, S3 E14, S4 E1, S4 E3 & S4 E4)

CHAPTER 7:
SEASON FOUR

DT kept chugging along with the arrival of Season 4. The animation style of the show's intro stayed the same, but a noticeable script change occurs.

We hear Josh narrate to us: "I'm Josh Gates. In my travels, I've seen some unexplainable things, and I've done some things I can't quite explain. Now, I've pulled together a team armed with the latest technology in the search for answers to the world's strangest mysteries. I'm not sure what's out there waiting for me, but I know what I'm looking for - the truth."

Season 4, Episode 1
Destinations: Italy & Kenya
Cases: Haunted Pompeii & Nandi Bear
Original Air Date: September 9th, 2010

Pompeii is a legend in the world of archaeology. The city reached its zenith in ancient times, amassing a population of about 11,000 around the year 80 BC. After a Roman invasion, it became ingratiated into its conquerer's culture until a very fateful day in the year 79 AD. Upon this day, the mighty Mount Vesuvius erupted and infamously buried the city in 20 feet of ash and fire. Each inhabitant was forever preserved in a chrysalis of ash - entombed and frozen in time, never to emerge.

Prior to their investigation of this fascinating site, the team makes a perilous rappel into a massive crater to retrieve a mystical rock that will enable them to contact the distressed spirits. They deploy the rock and conduct isolation sessions amongst the entombed dead in an effort to make contact. Pompeii may be frozen in time, but Team *DT*, with help from TAPS, are determined to prove there is still plenty of activity here.

Next, one of Africa's most notorious non-reptilian cryptids is the ferocious Nandi Bear. The beast is named after the Nandi tribe of western Kenya and is said to be a massive monster that is more canine than ursine. Worse, the creature is said to be fond of consuming human brains!

Josh, now a card carrying member of the Nandi Country Golf Club, leads the crew on a unique nighttime safari into the Kenyan wilderness. "Safe" from the confines of their off-road vehicle, the crew encounters very real African predators in the dark. Will they find evidence of the elusive Nandi Bear, or do they have real world jump scares during their ride?

Josh: "In a career filled with stupid activities, this is something special!"

Mike: "On a scale of 1-to-Scary, I'm about to [expletive] my pants."

Josh (on their car rental): "I can't win. Okay everybody, pile in! It's like something that fell out of a bag of Skittles."

Angkor Wat is a beautiful Cambodian shrine complex which holds the distinction of being the largest religious center in the world. The "City of Temples" was originally built as a Hindu shrine, but eventually converted to a Buddhist temple, becoming a national symbol of Cambodia. A location with such dynamic history is bound to harness energy and indeed, the site is reportedly haunted.

In an infamous pre-investigation moment, Josh encounters the "joy" of a skin-eating fish pedicure! With freshly exfoliated feet, he leads the team into the jungle temple. They prepare a special incense offering and witness strange anomalies. What is causing these mysteries and what lurks in the past of this religious Cambodian epicenter?

As Nessie is synonymous with Scotland and Champ is to New York State, so too is the Ogopogo in Canada. The snake-like beast is featured in myth of native Canadians from back in the 1800's. Predictably, the notoriety of Lake Okanagan's mystery denizen has been a major boon to cryptid pop culture. Suggested explanations range from mis-identification to comparisons in appearances to the Basilosaurus.

Lake Okanagan, a long and appropriately serpentine lake, is the venue of the second investigation in this episode. The team travels to British Columbia, specifically Rattlesnake Island, scanning the surrounding area in the air and beneath the chilly waters to see what exactly is disturbing the waters of the Great White North.

Josh: "This [car] is making some very weird noises." **Vanessa**: "Gates?"
Josh: "Yeah?" **Vanessa**: "This wheel's about to fall off."

Josh VO: "A day on bikes has left us all a little dusty." **Ali**: "I am filthy."
Josh: "Ali, did a tray of brownies just explode in your face?"

Josh: "I can drink my own pee. I just choose not to."

Josh VO: "Vancouver is ranked as one of the most livable cities in North America, which of course means we didn't stop there at all."

Season 4, Episode 3
Destinations: Japan & Tanzania
Cases: Haunted Haboro & the Mngwa
Original Air Date: September 23rd, 2010

Mining towns seem to be powerful catalysts for restless spirits and the abandoned town of Haboro is no different. The North Japanese island of Hokkaido plays host to this desolate ghost town, allegedly populated by the spirits of Japanese miners and enslaved Korean POW's.

It was literally a dark and stormy night that greeted the team as they constructed base camp amidst the ruined buildings. They focus their search on an old schoolhouse, paying heed to the warning of voracious bears on the prowl. Potentially paranormal evidence from their cold and dangerous night in the Far East is evaluated with the help of TAPS.

Next, Tanzania is an African country filled with large, apex predators, but there may be a very unnatural carnivore lurking on the Savannah's. The Mngwa is said to be a large, grey felid that is distinctly different from a lion in that it is quite a bit larger. In an interesting note, Mngwa attacks have been attributed to fellow Season 4 cryptid, the Nandi Bear, and vice versa!

It's another nighttime safari as the team hits the road to explore the dark corners of Africa. They cautiously make their way on foot, following a visit to a dry creek bed, looking for signs of life and abnormally large footprints. They collect some interesting evidence, but must make a hasty retreat when something begins stalking them in the darkness. This hunt for another of the world's mystery beasts may prove to be the most treacherous yet.

Josh: "You didn't like the sleeper train?" **Ali**: "I would have loved it, if I were four feet tall." **Josh**: "Are you a little tall for this country?" **Ali**: "A little tall for this country? I'm huge in Japan, and not in a good way."

Josh: "Bear! Ah! False alarm. Stuffed bear. False alarm." **Mike**: "God!" **Ali**: "I hate you, Josh."

Gabe: "Shawn - when it comes to man-on-man bunking, it's never too hot for pants."

Season 4, Episode 4
Destinations: Micronesia & Japan
Cases: Haunted Wrecks & the Kappa
Original Air Date: September 30th, 2010

In this very unique expedition, Josh and the team travel for the first time to the small atoll of Micronesia. Here, off the coast of Chuuk Island, lie the ruins of a Japanese stronghold left over from WWII. Many warships were sunk by coordinated US raids, leaving metallic, rusting leviathans and dangerous un-exploded ordinances behind. Seeking to prove that even the abyss cannot contain the dead, the team explores reports of apparitions and mystery sounds amongst the wrecks.

Josh embarks on a worldwide first, underwater paranormal investigation. The team pinpoints several key wrecks, diving into the briny deep to seek contact with the restless souls. Following this, they head inland to the island to look for land-lock spectres. With this unprecedented format, what will Team Truth come across?

You're familiar with the *Teenage Mutant Ninja Turtles*, right? Take away the color coded bandanas and pizza obsession, then you've essentially got the Kappa. These turtle-like water demons are both revered and feared throughout bodies of water in Japan. Mythology paints them as moody creatures, willing to assist humans with household chores, or just as likely to assault and drown them! They also feature a unique indentation on their heads, which must remain filled with water at all times, lest they perish.

Discounting the more folkloric interpretations, the *DT* crew casts a figurative net over Japan's lakes and rivers in search of a biological explanation. They don waders, scouring the marshland and caverns in their search. They also obtain certain evidence, which may help them uncover the identity of Japan's terrapin terror.

Josh VO: "The food offerings in Japan are also not for the faint of heart."
Josh: "The old pizza, potatoes, bacon, macaroni and cheese, clams casino, broccoli, shrimp, pasta dish." **Bobby**: "Yeah, that's the bathroom blow out platter."

Josh: "Oh Japan. You never cease to weird me out."

Translator: "It looked like [a] turtle. It looked like [a] ninja turtle." **Josh**: "Does it carry a samurai sword and love pizza?!"

Season 4, Episode 5
Destination: Russia
Case: Siberian Snowman
Original Air Date: October 7th, 2010

As we have seen before, the hairy hominoid sub-class is one of the most prolific of all cryptid types. Sightings have occurred from practically all walks of life and on nearly every nation on Earth. Of course, where does the existence of a large mystery primate seem more plausible than the inhospitable wastes of the frozen Siberian tundra?

A rare, full episode investigation takes Josh and the team into the frigid expanse to investigate sightings. Surviving impending danger from a local wolf pack, they turn up plenty of fascinating evidence. What results will they yield from their findings?

Josh: "It's beautiful out here! I can't feel any part of my face, but it's beautiful!"

Josh: "Just hang tight back there! You always complain you don't get enough time off. This is it. Bask in the sunshine out here. It's gotta be, what, 10, 12 degrees? Whoo!" **Mike**: "Worst boss ever." **Ali**: "Ever."

Season 4, Episode 6
Destinations: Kenya & Madagascar
Cases: Haunted Menengai & the Kalanoro
Original Air Date: October 14th, 2010

Menengai is a massive caldera (volcanic crater) located in the very cradle of humanity. Local Kenyans hold great relevance for the enormous geographical feature. Here, on the floor of the Great Rift Valley, is said to be the final dwelling space for the spirits of tribal warfare.

The 6-mile-wide pit will provide a challenging and unique expedition for the team. They descend into the darkness of the crater and prepare an offering to appease the spirits. What evidence will the team uncover, surrounded by the siren song of the natural and paranormal world?

Madagascar is an incredibly unique island off the South-Eastern coast of Africa. Having split off from the main continent, its flora and fauna have evolved exclusively in isolation. Perhaps the most unique creature on this island, if they in-fact exist, is the Kalanoro. These diminutive predators are said to have the unique feature of backwards facing feet, perhaps making them a distant cousin of the Alux. The dense jungle holds untold mysteries, so will the team discover an animal that would make Darwin balk?

Josh: "I'm an adventurous guy. I wear adventurous underwear."

Josh VO: "If there's one thing I've learned in my years of travel - every open air market in the world has at least one hippie with a bongo drum. On this occasion, he happened to be a member of our crew." **Gabe**: "Viva America! **Josh**: "Unbelievable. Somebody get this guy a hacky sack and a bottle of pachouli, please?"

Season 4, Episode 7
Destinations: Micronesia & Morocco
Cases: Nan Madol & the Succubus
Original Air Date: October 21st, 2010

Nan Madol is an ancient ruined city that lies on the island of Pohnpei in the western chain of the Micronesian atoll. The ruins are unique in that they feature a series of small islets broken up by various waterways. They are said to have directly influenced author HP Lovecraft in his Cthulhu mythos and according to locals, are powerfully haunted.

This is a unique investigation, in that it was suggested to the team by a *Destination Truth* viewer. The team leaps at the opportunity and travels from islet to islet, seeking contact through various EVP isolation sessions. In a frightening moment, Josh falls violently ill and relies on team medic Shawn to bring him back to strength. Is this the wrath of unsettled ghosts, and how will this affect their watery nighttime investigation?

A Succubus is a demonic entity, exclusively female. It seeks to lure men to their demise to extract their life force through sexual seduction. Jewish mythology dictates the first succubus as a woman named Lillith, Adam's wife before Eve, who engaged in a sexual tryst with an archangel. In Northern Africa, this age-old siren may stalk the desert regions, proving the tale expands beyond different cultures. Here, she is known as Aisha Kandisha and is said to be a centaur-like creature. She has the lower body of a bovine, specially a camel, but the upper torso of a buxom, topless temptress.

Team *DT* travels to Casablanca and ascend a hot air balloon to seek a possible dwelling for this mysterious she-demon. They discover an abandoned casbah and investigate the site. Will the team track down this female phantom, or will the men of Team Truth find themselves lost forever in the sands of Morocco's most famous city?

Josh VO: "Every week, we get dozens of emails from viewers asking us to explore some terrifying location. Sorry, Rick in Scottsdale. Your mother-in-law's house isn't the kind of place we're after!"

Josh: "Greatest car in *DT* history…for years I've been saying it. Take an old crappy truck, and a Tiki hut, and put them together. Finally, they listened!"

Josh: "I'd like to apologize for all the vomiting I did that night, guys."

Season 4, Episode 8
Destinations: Madagascar & Guam
Cases: Fangalobolo & the Taotao Mona
Original Air Date: October 28th, 2010

Madagascar will always play host to strange creatures, and our newest entry into the cryptid gallery is no different. This aerial beast is said to be akin to a colossal bat, but larger than the scientifically accepted largest bat, the flying fox. Said to roost in the dark caves of the island interior, it is perhaps another evolutionary anomaly in Madagascar's catalog of the odd.

The crew descends into the caves, braving swarms of smaller bats and a more dangerous menace: several hungry crocodiles. Will they uncover the truth behind this chiropteran menace? If there is indeed a mystery beast luring out there, Madagascar is surely the place to find it.

The Chamorro people of Guam tell tales of a type of spirit known as the Taotao Mona. They hold great reverence for this spirit, said to be very moody spectres of the past. These ghostly presences have been known to harass, abuse and curse those who they believe are treating their legacy poorly. Ironically, there have been some fan complaints after this aired that even the labeling of these spirits as "Guam Zombies" was incorrect.

Gabe accidentally disrupts a ceremonial cairn and Vanessa disturbs a sacred banyan tree, for which both are injured soon after, potentially giving credence to the irritable, vengeful nature of the spirits. Audio tech Mike is the next to feel their presence, as he is seemingly physically shoved out of an EVP session. These strange occurrences coupled with evidence add more pieces to this Pacific paranormal puzzle.

Josh: "These are the heads of cows with no bones in them. This is a stall apparently operated by Hannibal Lecter."

Josh VO: "You know what they say - it's not a Chamorro party until your paramedic winds up passed out on a water buffalo."

Josh: "I finally stumped you!" **Jim Dines**: "You have." **Josh**: "This is it! My dream in life has been to come down to this warehouse and have you not know what something is." **Jim**: "Mission accomplished." **Josh**: "I did it, finally!"

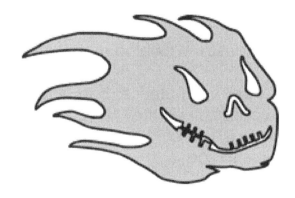

Season 4, Episode 9
- the DT Live Special
Destination: County Carlow Ireland
Cases: Ducketts Grove & Dunluce Castle Banshees
Original Air Date: March 17th, 2011

The Banshee, or Bean Sidhe, is a classic trope of celtic lore. She is exclusively a female spirit and is famous for her ear-splitting, keening cry. It is said that to hear the cry of the banshee is an omen of impending doom. Either the listener or someone they are connected to will surely end up dead, very soon.

She seems to particularly stalk members of eminent Irish families, which leads some to believe that the Banshee might actually be a summoned or cursed phantom. It is the modern day reports of the shrieking spirit that sends our team into action for a special Saint Patrick's Day investigation.

What follows is another important event in *DT* lore. For the first time, we are treated to a live investigation as the team scours the ruins of Duckett's Grove Castle in an unedited hunt for the paranormal. Joining them on this epic tour of Celtic lore are a host of guest investigators: Jael de Pardo, actress Allison Scagliotti and members of the *Ghost Hunters International* team.

The team encourages live viewer participation via the Banshee button at home from their computers and our eagle-eyed fellow fans manage to alert the team to several sightings. This episode proves to be one of the most interesting, unique and interactive journeys into the dark side of culture as our crew of explorers continue to scour the cursed haunt of Ireland's most famous spectre. No worries if you never saw it live - it's still on iTunes and Amazon for purchase as the abridged version!

Josh: "The question is not will we catch the Banshee - Ryder, can you go four hours on live TV without swearing?" **Ryder**: "I'll try my best."

Josh: "That's definitely a cow." **Barry**: "That'd be a sheep." **Josh**: "Sheep. Cow. Barnyard animal. Whatever."

Josh: "Rex, here's the important question - what's gonna kill me tonight?"

Josh: "Is your leg alright?" **Ryder**: "Yes." **Josh**: "Is it okay if I joke about it?"

Season 4, Episode 10
Destinations: Panama & Argentina
Cases: Haunted Island Prison & the Ucamar
Original Air Date: March 22nd, 2011

Coiba Island is a large, isolated piece of land off the coast of Panama in Central America. It is the largest island of the region and is generally a beautiful, picturesque nature preserve. Beneath the veneer though, lurks a sinister side.

A prison, established in the early 20th Century, played host to torture, murder and extreme unrest. The abandoned site is a blemish on the land and is said to be haunted by the phantasms of those who lost their lives in squalid condition. The team's investigation takes them into the bowels of the derelict penitentiary.

The Ucamar Zupai is an unusual cryptid in that it resembles your classic hairy hominoid, yet it retains bear-like characteristics, as well. This ursine beast has been sighted stalking Argentina, raiding garbage dumpsters in the area. This suggests it may be both a dangerous carnivore and an opportunistic forager. Plenty of livestock have fallen prey to the beast's deadly claws and teeth.

The crew takes off on horseback into the forests of the Andes Mountains. They deploy their new animal distress call simulator and seem to summon something in the night. What animal is lurking in the Andes, spooking the team's horses into a panic? Team Truth is determined to find out.

Josh: "Okay, just so I'm clear - you escaped a notorious Panamanian jungle island prison on a home made raft, is that correct? Alright, c'mon, up top! *high fives* That's pretty cool, I gotta hand it to you."

Rex: "There's something in there." **Ryder**: "No way! What do you mean?" **Rex**: "What the hell is that?" **Ryder**: "Like an animal?" **Rex**: "Yeah." **Ryder**: "What?!" **Rex**: "Whoa whoa, the water's moving." **Ryder**: "What is it? What is it?!" **Rex**: "Something's in there! Oh, it's a frog. *Mister Toad's Wild Ride.*" **Ryder**: "Damn it!"

Season 4, Episode 11
Destinations: Namibia & Panama
Cases: Haunted Mining Town & Dead Mystery Creature
Original Air Date: March 29th, 2011

The *DT* team has spent plenty of time investigating both Africa and haunted mining towns, so why not combine the two? Our destination is Kolmanskoppe, a mining community that was founded by German colonists. The country of Namibia has assimilated much of the European influence. After Ryder's memorable race against a wild ostrich, the team descends on the neighboring town of Luderite to begin their investigation.

Jael, possibly scarred from her harrowing experience in the Irish Banshee castle, returns to help the team scour the sands. With the team seemingly dropping one by one during the investigation, will they have the strength to continue their hunt for the paranormal?

Our next entry is unique in that it is not a cryptid that has been sighted for centuries, rather a confirmed, isolated incident. In 2009, an incident occurred in Panama in which a group of teens were allegedly attacked by a slimy, hairless, short-snouted, clawed creature. The beast attacked them in a river and the boys managed to not only slay the creature, but collected photographs of the corpse.

Josh and the team speak to the boys involved and the local Panamanian Emberá tribes. To them, the incident is not surprising, as they believe in the existence of an entire species of the creature. Determined to solve the mystery, they investigate the nearby Chagres National Park. They explore the caves and rivers of the area to explore the various explanations offered for the hairless creature's existence.

Josh: "Look at that. Wild ostriches. One of the fastest animals in the world."
Ryder: "I don't think they're that fast." **Josh**: "Ryder, stop trying to race every animal in the world. You are not faster than an ostrich." **Jael**: "I bet Ryder's faster than an ostrich." **Ryder**: "Let me out of this car!"

Josh: "Jael, this proves that you're not a crazy person." **Jael**: "Well, I think you're a crazy person for locking me in a butcher's freezer." **Josh**: "Proves that, too! It proves both of those things."

Josh VO: "In 2009, a mysterious creature came out of nowhere and created massive, international buzz. No, not Justin Bieber."

Season 4, Episode 12
Destinations: Thailand & Namibia
Cases: Giant Ghosts & Night Stalker
Original Air Date: April 5th, 2011

Josh and the team have embarked on many ghost investigations, but these spirits tend to generally be your garden-variety human sized spectres. In Southeast Asia, they grow them big! There are tales of the Phi Pret, spirits held in the underworld as a result of a sinful life. They are damned to a tortuous afterlife, as their mouths are too tiny to provide sustenance, resulting in a rail-thin frame. Oh, and they also happen to be 30 feet tall!

Thailand is the venue and the Phanom Rung temple is the site. Utilizing intriguing video evidence, the team sets up base camp and proceeds with their investigation. Odd physical evidence and an assault on one of the team members contribute to the case as Team Truth patrols the ruins for signs of these massive, hungry damned souls.

The Night Stalker is one of the more obscure and elusive of the creatures investigated by Team Truth. The beast seems to be an amalgam of feline, canine and hominid characteristics. It's predatory tactics are actually very familiar. Livestock turning up drained of blood suggests that somebody smuggled El Chupacabra over to Africa in a doggy carrier!

The expedition to South West Africa begins with the graphic analysis of a slaughtered giraffe. As night falls, they head out into the Etosha National Park, joined by the late arrival of frequent guest Jael de Pardo. They encounter an abandoned village and a freshly killed goat, so what strange creature stalks the Savannah's of Namibia and can the team track down the deadly carnivore?

Josh VO: "We carried Ryder to a nearby farm house, where Rex began treatment." **Rex**: "You got two really good abrasions." **Josh VO**: "The team stood by Ryder and offered moral support." **Ryder**: "Ow! You didn't say that was gonna hurt. You have to warn me! Give me something to bite on. Josh? Did you ever get that coordination amulet for me?" **Josh**: "No I didn't, but I really wish we looked harder for it."

Josh: "This is the kind of market where I turn around and Rex has bought something really ridiculous."

Season 4, Episode 13
Destinations: Thailand & Cyprus
Cases: Tree People & the Ayia Napa Monster

The myth of the Naree Pon (or "Nariphon") holds distinct roots in Buddhist mythology. According to the tale, a powerful deity named Indra crafted trees that would bear fruit resembling women that were designed to distract a host of lustful vagabonds. The would-be sexual assaulters would then be distracted by the shapely tree nymphs, thus granting Indra's wife safe passage through the orchards to gather fruit. In Thailand, these plant-women hybrids have breached the veil of myth, thanks to two shriveled corpses housed in Wat Ampawan, a Buddhist temple.

The team's expedition takes them into the Thai forest as they hunt for these Asian anomalies. They encounter various shrines (including one dedicated to their old friend, the Ninki Nanka) and plenty of creepy crawlers as they explore the caverns of the region. What mysteries will the temple bodies unlock and what will Team *DT* find deep in the Thai jungle?

Ayia Napa is the name of a section of land near Cape Greko, located on the island of Cyprus. This island is the most populated one in the Mediterranean region and, as with most of the area, holds strong ties to Greek culture and mythology. It is this diverse culture that may have given rise to a large serpentine beast sighted off the coastal waters, which is the focus of the episode's second half. Descriptions vary but one standard remains that the creature is aggressive and carnivorous.

Team *DT* embarks to the picturesque island and conducts a daytime investigation of the coastal caves. They later head below the waves for a good old fashioned nighttime aquatic search. What evidence will they turn up with their trust ROV camera? Can they deduce exactly what is stalking the waters of the Mediterranean?

Josh: "Ryder, remember that time on The Great Wall where you flipped upside down? Don't do that." **Ryder**: "Oh boy." **Josh**: "There you go. You got it, Ryder." **Ryder**: "You didn't have a lot of faith in me." **Josh**: "I had a lot of faith in you. I knew you were gonna come down. I just thought you were gonna come down a lot faster, upside down, screaming. Ryder made it down here safe! Rex, I owe you five bucks!"

Josh VO: "Finally, we picked up a few items for future use." **Josh**: "This is a cane! It's got a flash light, a compass. This is for Season 19, where Ryder and I are just hobbling along."

Season 4, Episode 14
Destination: Antarctica
Case: Haunted, Abandoned Stations
Original Air Date: April 19th, 2011

Antarctica is of course, the southernmost land mass, sitting on the very bottom of the Earth. The frozen continent spreads out over 5 Million square miles and is essentially a barren wasteland. Now, Team Truth will embark on an unprecedented, history-making voyage to the ice encrusted desert. Their destination: Deception Island, located off the northwestern horn of the continent. This nearly enclosed caldera is home to a multitude of abandoned, haunted British research stations.

Harrowing experiences in the compound and a derelict graveyard prove taxing to the team, both mentally and physically. A second research station on the main land mass known as the Wordie House is the destination for phase two. Plenty of bumps in the perennial twilight greet the team as they scour the isolated structures. This journey into the frozen wastes of the most desolate place on Earth will weigh heavily on the team as they attempt to unearth the arctic anomalies at the bottom of the world.

Ryder: "You guys do something different with your hair?" **Josh**: "Oh, you know, Tony and I are sporting our sweet, Arctic beards."

Josh: "Car's got a pretty sweet horn."

Josh VO: "Since our journey would be perilous, we stepped into a local outfitter for critical, cold weather gear." **Josh**: "Alright guys, we gotta pick up supplies. We gotta pick up food. We need the leather jacket from *Thriller*. "

Josh: "I want my bra back! I WANT MY BRA BACK!"

SEASON FOUR MILESTONES:

- **S4 E1** - First paranormal investigation of Pompeii EVER
- **S4 E4** - First underwater paranormal investigation EVER
- **S4 E9** - *DT Live* Special with guest investigators Kris Williams of *Ghost Hunters International*, Barry Fitzgerald also of *GHI*, and Allison Scagliotti of *Warehouse 13,* as well as many *DT* crew members from mixed Seasons appear
- **S4 E11** - Jael de Pardo introduced as "guest" investigator for this episode, since she was then on *Fact or Faked*. Also, *Bass Pro Shops* premieres as another sponsorship
- **S4 E12** - Jael "guest" investigates again
- **S4 E14** - First paranormal investigation of Antarctica EVER

CHAPTER 8:
DT FANS

I remember the day we were all told *DT* was not coming back. I saw it coming, but it was still a tough pill to swallow.

A couple of years prior, I was hanging out with Josh before he was to speak at the LA Times Travel Show convention. He said the words you didn't ever want to hear as a fan - "One day, *DT* will be over" - but you can still be in denial and think "well, it isn't right now." I just gave him a dismissive wave and said we would all cross that bridge when we come to it.

I was also really sick that trip, so I chalked it up to being delusional from lack of sleep and feeling like crap. Yay, denial.

Fast forward to March 27th, 2014 - I was just coming off a job interview and was killing time on my computer at Starbucks waiting to meet a friend. Then, there it was - the announcement from Josh confirming that *DT* was officially over. This was made even more real by the email Josh sent me shortly after - "Thank you so much for all your tireless work on behalf of *DT*. Seriously. You're a rock star. Onward and upward from here, kid. Exciting things are afoot."

Okay. What now? I was wondering what was going to happen next. I could only imagine how Josh, the production company and the rotating cast felt about this. In the middle of typing up a heartfelt statement to fellow fans, I got a mystery call on my phone. Was it about the job interview I just did?

Some fellow fans I supported on a *Walking Dead* fan-run podcast called *Walker Stalkers* surprise ambushed me - they loved a question I submitted for one of their shows and Andrew Lincoln (AKA Rick Grimes) was calling me to answer that same fan question! For once, I was the befuddled fan on the other line of the phone. We had a great conversation about method acting and religion that I will never forget.

This moment was not only exciting, but it rejuvenated me. I remembered the thrill of being that fan behind the scenes, helping make things like this happen for other fans. How many lives of others did I help make better, or just a little more exciting, running the fan site, *DT Fan Radio* and my YouTube channel with exclusive videos for my fellow fans from conventions and events? Everything would be okay, I told myself.

On April 2nd, a little while after that day which would live an infamy for *DT* fans, I received another Josh email. Two words inside: "I'm baaaaack:" followed by the press release about *Expedition Unknown*. Nothing golden can stay, but just like the seasons, the things we enjoy come back to us in new forms. I was just glad to still be part of the adventure!

In this chapter, I want to highlight my fellow fans who made *DT* the exciting phenomena that it was. I also provide a timeline of *DT Fan Radio* specials with cast members and the dates they aired in **Acknowledgements**.

KAT SANZO of Florida, USA. *Favorite Cases*: **Ninki Nanka, both Hoia Biachu episodes, & Chernobyl.** Josh Gates is a funny, tell it like it is, no holds-barred host. If ever there was a person to bring the paranormal and unexplained into the mainstream media, Josh is the person I would choose - easy to understand, relatable, and HILARIOUS.

The day I won free tickets to his show in Rhode Island really changed my life. I had always been a huge fan of *Destination Truth* and that day I happened across a Twitter feed offering tickets to a show I wouldn't have been able to go to otherwise. I was visiting family up North and, luckily, my brother was crazy enough to come with me, since he was driving me over from Connecticut.

Vine videos were a particularly new thing at the time and I was trying to figure out how to make an awesome Vine at a Dunkin Donuts when Amanda dropped a bomb - we were going to get to meet Josh. I decided, along with the help of the group of us going to meet him, that I would make a video about how awesome it would be to actually BE Josh Gates - traveling the world and solving mysteries!

Josh turned out to be a VERY cool guy and I was so starstruck that he had done my video with me! From that day, I still have good friends from the people I met and I watch everything that has Josh in it.

PHILLIP CHU of New York, USA. *Favorite Cases*: **Suicide Forest, Hoia Baciu Forest & Ghosts of Masada.** The reason why I watched and enjoyed *Destination Truth* was because of the variety of subjects they've explored. It was definitely one of my favorite shows on TV, as my Wednesday nights were anchored with *Ghost Hunters* and *DT*.

It was exciting to meet and chat with Josh at his book signing inside the NBC store and to also have my photo taken with him, and this was actually my second time meeting Josh. The first time was back in 2010 when he hosted the *Ghost Hunters* special live 100th episode from 30 Rock.

VACATION WITH JOSH GATES
A SONG BY FAN DAVID RITTER

LET'S GO VACATION WITH
THE JOSH GATES
WE CAN SEARCH FOR YETI
AND THE LIKE

THERE'S A DESTINATION TRUTH HIDDEN
ON THE OTHER SIDE OF THE DIKE

I WANT TO SEE EL CHUPACABRA
SOMEWHERE IN A TOWN
I CAN'T PRONOUNCE
THERE'S A MONSTER ABOUT TO POUNCE
BRING ON THAT MONSTER ANIMATION

THERE'S A DESTINATION TRUTH INSIDE HERE
WHAT THE HELL'S THAT GROWLING
IN THE BUSHES?
KEEP YOUR WITS ABOUT YOU SO
IT DOESN'T, DOESN'T, EAT YOU

THERE'S NO WAY THAT
WE CAN PASS HERE
BETTER CRACK OUT
THE RAPPELLING GEAR
WAIT WHAT'S THAT HOWLING
IN THE DISTANCE?
DID YOU GET ANYTHING ON THE FLIR?

WHY DO WE ALWAYS GET SCREWED
WITH TRUCKS?
WHERE ARE THE ROADS CAUSE NOW
WE'RE STUCK?
HEY CHECK THESE SCRATCHES ON
THIS BIG TREE
LET'S MAKE A CAST ON THE GROUND

THERE'S A DESTINATION TRUTH
INSIDE HERE
WHAT THE HELL'S THAT GROWLING
IN THE BUSHES?
KEEP YOUR WITS ABOUT YOU SO IT
DOESN'T, DOESN'T, EAT YOU
KEEP YOUR WITS ABOUT YOU SO IT
DOESN'T EAT YOU

HIS SITE IS *MACMUFASA.COM*

DRAWING BY:

JESSICA MITCHELL of CANADA
Favorite Case: Bermuda Triangle

KENT HOLLOWAY of Florida, USA. *Favorite Cases*: **Icelandic Elves, Island of the Dolls, Bermuda Triangle & the Yeti.** *Primal Thirst*, the first book in *The ENIGMA Directive* thriller series, all started with one thought in mind: "Wouldn't it be cool if there was a book out there similar to the adventures that the *DT* crew had on a weekly basis?"

So, after a considerable amount of timing in searching for this great non-existent book (this, of course, was before Amazon and e-Readers opened the world up to the amazing fiction being released by indie authors from all around the world), I decided to do something about it. *The ENIGMA Directive* featured the adventures of world renowned cryptozoologist Dr. Obadiah "Jack" Jackson and his team of highly skilled researchers (and one by-the-book US Army Ranger) as they traveled the world hunting for cryptids.

During the course of marketing my *ENIGMA Directive* novels, I had the great fortune to get to know several of the *Destination Truth* team. I interviewed the lovely and hilarious Erin Ryder for my blog on multiple occasions. I enjoyed getting to chat with Josh on Amanda's *DT Fan Radio* show about my book, as well. I also grew very close to Rex Williams and even became his co-administrator for his Facebook fan page, and this relationship eventually led to one of the greatest days of my life.

As I grew closer to Rex and his wife Michele, I soon found myself getting to know Gabe Copeland and his fiancé (at the time) Bridget. A friendship quickly developed among all five of us and when the time came for Gabe's and Bridget's big day, I couldn't believe it when I was asked to perform their wedding ceremony, since I am an ordained Baptist minister.

It was a fan's dream come true. These two people make such a wonderful couple. I've grown to love them, plus Rex and his wife, like my own family. I am truly blessed to have been able to be part of theirs.

KIM KNOX of Massachusetts, USA. *Favorite Cases*: **Ghosts of the Great Wall, Israeli Mermaid & the two Yeti episodes.** Aside from personal interests in the paranormal, Josh's narration and humor kept me watching *Destination Truth* at first. As the show evolved, I saw that it was so much more than the investigations, or about "finding something" in the way of definitive proof of the thing they were investigating. It was about the places, the people and their stories.

Eventually, I felt I just had to meet the lady behind *Singularity Fan Pages* and treat her to lunch. That first time that Amanda and I met up in Boston, the weather was dreadful, but we are Truthies! So we trekked on and had a great afternoon out together. It was an unforgettable beginning to a good friendship that would grow over the years. In fact, several fellow Truthies have become good friends over the years and we all met through Amanda's fan work. Also in 2013, I finally got to meet Josh Gates in person. That was one of the most FAN-tastic days of my life.

BARBARA PERRY of New York, USA. Favorite Cases: Pompeii, Chernobyl, Alien Mummies & Doll Island. We stumbled upon the show while scrolling through the channels waiting for our son Matthew to come home from his first day at a new school. It was a DT marathon! The show was about the Yeren, so we knew we had to show Matthew, who is a huge fan of all things cryptid.

It's significant to mention that Matthew is on the autism spectrum. He's scientific and literal rather then logical. Josh Gates and Destination Truth gave him a sense of belonging, that he isn't weird or crazy; confirmation from an intelligent, revered person, that he is not alone in the belief and search for these legends. This brought out emotions and dialogue from Matthew we had not seen before and continues to do so to this day.

How often does a parent get to witness their child meet their idol? It was a very emotional day for me. My daughter, Kelsey, also drew a picture for Josh. Matthew, always needing something to hold onto to give him comfort in an unfamiliar situation, brought along his Disney Wall-E plush doll. I begged him to let me hold it while he spoke with Josh. He refused. When we walked up to the table to meet Josh, after saying hello to us and asking the kids their names, Josh commented on Wall-E and how he was one of his favorites!

To this day, I'm sure Josh Gates has no idea of the impression he has left on my son, my daughter and in my heart. He loves his fans and it was evident.

"To this day, I know Josh Gates has no idea of the impression he has left on my son, my daughter, and my heart" -Barbara from NY

Art Work by Jen Street from Texas. Favorite case: Island of the Dolls. Her website is JenStreet.com

BRAD ACEVEDO of California, USA. *Favorite Cases*: **The Suicide Forest, the Hoia Baciu forest & the Valley of the Kings.** I've always had a fascination with the paranormal and the mysterious. Couple this with my love for the natural world and an admiration for all things cryptozoological was the next logical step.

I do indeed owe a lot to *Destination Truth* and the mysterious world of the unknown. My fandom of the show was the very catalyst that led to the initial meeting between me and my beloved (one Amanda Rosenblatt, your intrepid tour guide through the landscape that is the very book you are reading). I have also formed warm memories of interactions and conversations with Josh and other *DT* personalities such as Erin Ryder and Brad Kuhlman. Partaking in the humorous and exciting adventures of the *DT* team also helped set my mind on track when I tragically lost my Mom to leukemia.

So yeah, *DT* has been a pretty important part of my life, surpassing the status of merely being "a show that I enjoy". It has lead me to love, helped me through dark times and aided me to indulge in an undying fascination.

There is so much to be seen, to be discovered out there in the vast world. The investigations may have ended, but the call to adventure looms ever more prominent in those who would seek the truth.

MENDY HODSON-YOCHUM of Missouri, USA. *Favorite Cases*: **Island of the Dolls, Antarctica, & the Suicide Forest.** I fell in love with *Destination Truth* because of its ability to let me explore the world beyond my front porch, along with the secrets and treasures that are hidden among its inhabitants. I am thankful to *DT* not just for the love of travel that it inspired in me, but for the friendships that blossomed from it. I have made some lifelong friends that support and truly care for one another. We may have started out as a *DT* family, but we evolved into so much more.

I was never able to meet any of the cast of *DT* in person, but on social media, Erin Ryder always inspires me to do the best that I can do, and Rex Williams checks in on my progress for nursing school. There were a few occasions on *DT Fan Radio* that I was granted the privilege of conversing with Josh Gates. I don't think I ever got over my fear of speaking to him, but I always loved being able to pick his brain about travel or the possibility of another adventurous tales-in-traveling book from him.

ERIKA SCHAEFER of Washington State, USA. Josh Gates is the "guy next door" on the show. He's the crazy neighbor with all the insane stories of getting drunk with tribesmen and coming face-to-face with deadly forces of all kinds, and you are sure he's 99% full of crap. But watching *Destination Truth* allows you go to along in the passenger seat, be there for the shenanigans, and realize that crazy neighbor guy is actually telling the truth (no pun intended)! I love the investigations, but some of my favorite moments have been when the team is traveling to the location. It's always awesome to see what Tiki Bar Mobile or Convertible Airplane they will get stuck with this episode!

Josh on fans of the show and on the fan site, via a *DT Fan Radio* episode: "We really like to think of *DT* as the little show that could. It's on a bit late, it's on at 10, and we are really fortunate to have *Ghost Hunters* in front of us because they're very much the wind at our sails. But it's a really ambitious show for what it costs to make it. The fact of the matter is that it's one of the most international shows on TV, which is a fact we sort of figured out a long the way. We end up touching down in more countries in this season than *Amazing Race*, and that's amazing because we make this show with a very lean group of people. It's really gratifying to have folks supporting it, and obviously all the work you do at the website, but all the fans calling and stuff like that. We really appreciate it, in fact, it really means a lot to us."

KRISTIN GDULA of LOUISIANA, USA. At eight years old, we had a school project to make a bucket list of things we wanted to do when we grew up. My classmates wrote things like "become a Nascar driver" and "have a family". Some lists went on for whole pages. My list was one line: "Climb Mt. Kilimanjaro." Somehow, the idea stuck. As I grew through high school, I debated taking a gap year and climbing Kili before going to college. The finances weren't there for me to do both, and I chose education. I vowed to make the journey before my 27th birthday. I was going to have adventures. I was going to see the world.

(some) FAN ♥ PHOTOS

KRISTIN'S STORY CONTINUED: Something happens to you when you hear the word "cancer" in a doctor's office. Some people bounce back from this news pretty quickly and fight hard. Some, like me, sink hard and fast into an awful, deep, soul crushing depression. My bucket list at that moment had drastically shifted, but was another one liner: "be alive". For years, I had been suffering with chronic fatigue and other symptoms that I couldn't figure out. Well, eventually the cancer reared its ugly head enough to be diagnosed. My thyroid had to go.

That's about the time when I saw my first episode of *DT*. It was the first episode of Season 2 "The Yeti" where Josh and company head to Nepal to search for Bigfoot. I think I mostly watched it because I couldn't find the remote to change the channel, but Nepal caught my attention mainly because of Mt. Everest. It was a small glimmer an a dark time. I didn't know it then, but it was my first step in coming out of my messy, smelly, lonely cocoon (AKA my apartment) and becoming me again.

Week after week, I fought my disease and week after week, I tuned into *DT*. I went outside more often. I ate real food instead of day-old pizza. I started talking to people, including on social media, and that included Amanda. She was the head of fan relations for *DT* and was as good a friend as I could have.

She had me on her radio show and I asked Josh about climbing Kili. It was the first time I'd talked about it in a long time. She and I camped out together for a few hours waiting to get our copies of Josh's book signed. I think I got a little tongue tied and didn't say very much. How do you sum up a crazy story like mine in a few seconds? She stayed a true friend through my recovery and still remains so to this day.

I'm not saying *DT* saved my life. If it hadn't been a crazy show on TV, it would have eventually been something. What I *am* saying is that it rekindled in me a sense of adventure that had been long slumbering, and deeply needed.

I went from living minute-to-minute to having a plan many years down the road. Josh Gates, *DT*, and a sense that adventure is always out there have prodded me back to my goal. Kili still stands tall and proud. And so do I.

THERESA BRUNDAGE of Pennsylvania, USA. *Favorite Case*: **the Ropen**. I've been a fan of *Destination Truth* from its first season in 2007, and Josh Gates is definitely the reason. He brings a bit of healthy skepticism and snarky humor to the show that no one else could. The most entertaining episodes are when he is interacting with locals and the other cast members. I could never pick one favorite episode, but I have several favorite scenes. During the search for the Ropen in Season 1 on episode 3, his conversation with Max the guide makes me laugh no matter how many times I watch it. The Japanese Haunted Forest and the Island of the Dolls gave me chills and really showed that Josh cares for his team. As much as I enjoy *Expedition Unknown*, *Destination Truth* was the original and had a winning formula.

JUSTIN WANAMAKER of Massachusetts, USA. *Favorite episode*: **DT Live from Ireland**. In August of 2013, I was one of a lucky few people to have the pleasure of meeting Josh Gates. I started the day off by meeting up with my cousin Amanda to go and meet some other *Destination Truth* fans a few hours before the start of the Josh Gates show. We got together and swapped stories on how we became fans of *DT*. It was then that we found out from Amanda that she was able to get Josh to come out before the show and meet us for about 15 minutes.

Now let me tell you all that I have met many famous people, from sports icons to TV show and Movie stars, and Josh was one of the nicest people I have ever met. He came out to the lobby of the theater he would later be speaking at inside of, and spoke to a small group of us. A few of us gave him gifts - nothing huge, but small tokens of our love for the show. I personally make custom trading cards for people I meet and made one for Josh to keep and one to sign. When it was my turn for a short 1-on-1 with Josh, I gave him the custom card. His reaction was great. He was excited and said "Wow, I have my own baseball card! Thank you"

For him to like something simple but with thought into it made him one of my favorite people. After another 10 minutes or so and him making a short Vine video with one of the others in the group, he was off to get ready for the show. After that, we were all still excited from meeting and finding out one of the people you admire is really as nice as he seems on TV, and we all went to eat at a divey but great buffet together while we waited for the show. Seemed appropriate to the culinary adventures they had on *DT*.

The show he did later did not disappoint. He told many stories, showed a few videos and took some fan questions. Well, it occurred to me after meeting him, that I forgot to ask my question. It was time for him to wrap up when one of his people with the microphone said I had raised my hand since the start of the question period.

I got to ask the last question of the night and it was if he could explore any place on Earth, where would it be. He said it was a great question, and the ocean would be his, as it is one of the largest still unknown portions of the Earth not explored. In closing, I think Josh is one of the most genuine people on the planet and he knows without us, he wouldn't be where he is.

TAMMY FELTON of Alabama, USA. *Favorite Case*: **Hoia Bochu Forest**. What do I love most about *DT*? It really wasn't so much about the actual investigations, but the interviews and research the *DT* team did. I love how they took us into the culture of the town/city/village they were visiting. No matter how crazy some of the claims or people were, Josh still treated them with respect and listened to their stories. We were welcomed into their homes and they shared pieces of their lives with us.

DT taught me that when you travel, you shouldn't be a tourist, but [rather] a visitor. Meet the locals, listen to their stories, eat where they eat, ask them where you should go to learn about the culture and who they are, why they live and believe the way they do. Josh and *DT* taught me it isn't about the destination, but the journey that takes you there.

JASMINE MAE WITH of Ohio, USA. *Favorite Case*: **Chernobyl.** In 2011, I had started posting vlogs on my Youtube channel (Jamiestarr319a) vlogging about my favorite show, *Ghost Adventures*, which you all may know is a paranormal investigation show that airs on the Travel Channel. Amanda found me, since she was already a fan of paranormal shows, and asked to interview me for her fan podcast series. After that interview, we became friends over our love of paranormal shows.

When I started following her on social media, it in turn led to me following

Josh Gates from *DT* and checking it out. In fact, I even got to talk to Josh on the phone when Amanda had him on-air for an interview, and I also got to meet Josh at the Lexington, Kentucky Scarefest convention.

It's great to be part of a community that supports similar interests and I'll always be thankful for the connections I've made through my favorite television shows, actors, and singers.

DAVID RITTER of Oklahoma, USA. Writer of the song "Vacation with Josh Gates" - I love all kinds of things [related to] searching for monsters, the unexplained, etc. It's right up my alley. I naturally gravitated towards *DT*. Josh's personality, his sense of humor, that just sealed the deal for me. I really loved the Chernobyl case, but any episode where Josh and the gang hang out with the locals or the market always struck my fancy.

CELEBRITY FANS OF DT

Destination Truth was a hit with everyone - especially to Josh's peers on the Syfy network! Among some of the bigger fans was Colin Ferguson of *Eureka*, who sat down with the fan site once to talk about how he wanted to be on the show.

In various interviews with the fan site, many of Josh's fellow Syfy Channel costars had stated they would want to be on *DT*. Joanne Kelly and Eddie McClintock from *Warehouse 13* must have been jealous that their costar Allison got to be on *DT*, but Saul Rubinek of the same show stated with humor "they can't afford me," when asked if he ever wanted to be on the show. Amanda Tapping and Robin Dunne of Syfy's *Sanctuary* also stated they wanted to be on the show, and it doesn't stop there.

"I have asked him to get me on *DT*," **Colin Ferguson of Syfy's *Eureka* said in an interview with the fan site.** "We've been talking about that forever. Problem is, he's got such a flight thing that it's his story, so he can keep his story…it's too hard to sort it out, but we're going to. We have to!"

WOW!

Fan art by Brandt Kofton of the USA.

Marc Tetlow

The line to see @SteveGonsalves1 @davetango @joshuagates @erinRyder13 at 11:30 in the Sheraton ball room!

Co-author of this book with Josh & Ryder at SDCC 2011

Custom Josh Funko with Hamburger Earmuffs by Michelle Strickland, USA

Art by Steven Anthony Adams of Ohio, USA.

Surprisingly, Colin got to do another cameo instead of *DT*, but he said "I got burned on *Ghost Hunters* because I go to San Francisco to do *GH*, right? Then, the network is all of the sudden like, 'That's a great idea! Let's send [Allison] Scagliotti to Chile.' So, she gets to go to freakin' Chile, and I get to go to San Francisco?! It's like, oh okay, that's cool. So yeah, I'd love to be on *Destination Truth*."

THE FAN SITE HELPERS

I have had some lovely people help me out with the fan pages over the years with research and admin assistance on my social media pages, and I wanted to highlight a couple of them here. I also mention all the folks I can remember in the **Acknowledgements** section of this book.

MICHELLE STRICKLAND of South Carolina, USA. *DT* really hooked me around the start of Season Two. I had just joined Twitter a few months before, followed Josh Gates and Amanda's fan run Twitter handle for the fan community, and made many an online friend of Truthies. I had a great experience running a side *DT* group and still use much of that knowledge with my new *Expedition Unknown* group covering Josh's newest endeavor. Though *DT* is now over, the old friendships have endured. For me, *DT* lives on in custom Funko Pop Vinyl recreations that I have made.

AISLYNN TURNBULL of Germany. I began watching *DT* almost a decade ago. The incredible locations are what snagged my attention, but it was the humor that kept me coming back. While living in Japan, I began to get into the show more and started researching it online. One of the searches lead me to a fan page on Facebook, and I was impressed with Amanda's dedication to the show and to her fellow fans. Through this page, I was even contacted by one if *DT's* cast members! I was pretty tickled.

CHAPTER 9:
SEASON FIVE

Season Five of *DT* came in with a roar. The return of our show came back with serious adrenaline and even the season premiere was two new episodes stacked on top of each other in the same night. We saw the return of past cast members, a revisit to an old location and some awesome new cases.

As far as changes, we also were treated to a change in the show's intro animation. We sweep through the deep jungle in the night to see the *DT* logo sitting on top of what looks like ancient ruins. The shot then transfers over to a night vision view, paying homage to all the investigations requiring use of this device.

While it is very sad that this is the final batch of episodes for this great show, they were also truly some of the best ones we ever saw. Talk about unofficially going out with a bang!

Season 5, Episode 1
Destination: Vietnam
Case: Batutut
Original Air Date: July 10th, 2012

The Batutut is our next member of the infamous, hairy hominid family. Also known as the Ngooi Rung ("Forest Man"), this ape man has been sighted in both Vietnam and Laos. In an interesting twist, soldiers in the Vietnam War actually sighted the beast, making this perhaps the first cryptid spotted on wartime battlefields. It has been described as a six foot tall, reddish furred hominid, making it a similar cousin of Sasquatch or perhaps a larger species of orangutan.

The prime habitat for this mystery primate is the large, cave-riddled Phong Nha-Kẻ Bàng National Park along the North East coast of Vietnam. This trek turns out to be particularly treacherous - the full episode investigation pits them against snakes, rapids and plenty more dangers. The team's second night in Ke Bang takes them further into the jungle, where they make a fascinating discovery. If they can make it out of the jungle in one piece, they will emerge with some of the best evidence yet acquired.

Josh VO: "Despite the heat, the market turned out to have something for everyone. Richie bravely tried the street meat." **Richie**: "You wanna try a little escargot?" **Josh**: "You're gonna escar-GO to the bathroom in a few minutes!"

Ryder: "You gotta steer it! That's what those horns are for." **Josh**: "Ow! [expletive] you. You do that again and I swear to [expletive], I will turn you into a steak. I am [expletive] around! Go." **Ryder**: "He's like the water buffalo whisperer. Good job!"

Ryder: "Somebody get me a piece of paper - I wanna write my will real quick!"

Season 5, Episode 2
Destinations: Romania & Belize

Our next episode comes to us via popular fan demand, as Team *DT* returns to the infamous Hoia Baciu Forest in Romania. As we've seen previously in the Season 3 premiere, this dark patch of land is perpetually and powerfully paranormally charged. Just as before, an attempted aerial recon ends in near disaster, forcing Josh to travel by land into the dense, dark forest.

Former camera man Evan B. Stone returns to face his fears, following his earlier incident in this area. Indeed, the team witnesses more activity before the official investigation even begins. For perhaps the first time, the team is forced to call a tactical retreat due to the onslaught of the unknown. With the spilling of blood, the team finds themselves hunted once again in one of the most terrifying places in the world.

Turning out to be an unprecedented new cryptid sub-class, the backwards footed gremlin is our next case! This is our third member of the unusual family, following the Alux and Kalanoro, which suggests either a genetic link or a folkloric connection.

The Tata Duende stalks the land of Central America, specifically the country of Belize. It is close to being a North American leprechaun, as sightings offer a distinctive outfit of a red suit plus a hat, and the makings of a trickster sprite. It's name translates to "Grandfather Demon", further fueling the fires of an old world legend.

Team Truth journeys to the Central American jungle in search of this minuscule menace. They decide to take a biological approach to this story and encounter plenty of all-too-real reptilian dangers. Will the team manage to track down the latest in their catalog of backwards-footed beasties?

Josh VO: "I reached out to my former cameraman Evan to see if he'd return to the scariest location in *Destination Truth* history." **Josh**: *on the phone* "Evan, it's Josh." **Evan**: "How ya doin'?" **Josh**: "Listen buddy, I got two words for ya - haunted forest." *dial tone* **Josh**: "Hello?"

Josh: "Our next stop is Professor Adrian Patrut. He's the real authority of the haunted forest. We interviewed him last time. Hopefully he hasn't cut that sweet hair of his."

Josh: "Ryder, can you Belize we're here?" **Ryder**: "I know, it's un-Belize-able." **Kyle**: "We are not doing that!" **Josh:** "Oh yes, we are. You better Belize it! The whole trip. Starts now."

Season 5, Episode 3
Destinations: Fiji & Philippines
Cases: Ghosts of Cannibal Victims & the Kapre
Original Air Date: July 17th, 2012

The city of Suva is located on Viti Levu Island on the Fiji island chain. It is generally a beautiful city with a bit of a dark past. Located nearby is the village of Nabutautau, infamous for playing host to the slaughter and consumption of Reverend Thomas Baker. Baker was a missionary who became a victim and meal for the cannibalistic residents of the village in the

19th Century. As one would expect, the village is now home to a collection of restless spirits of both the villagers and victims of cannibalism.

Team Truth acquires special permission from a contemporary (and non-cannibal identifying) Tribal Chief to explore a cavern that was said to have acted as a giant cooking oven. They head further into the unoccupied portion of the village and conduct isolation sessions, as they attempt to contact Baker and the spirits of any other past victims. An eerie appearance of a strange substance and a physical experience by Ryder all contribute to a disturbing night in the Fijian jungle.

We head back to the Philippines for our next investigation, looking for a cryptid that sounds like he'd be a fun hangout in a bar or pub. According to folklore, the Kapre is an 8-foot-tall hairy hominid clad in a loincloth. He perpetually smokes a cigar and possesses a stone that grants wishes! On a more biological basis, the creature is likely a large predatory beast that most likely does not have emphysema, nor grant wishes if you repeat his magic words.

Before their hunt, Josh and Ryder re-encounter the infamous Balut delicacy, so rather than lose their lunch again, the team travels inland to the Philippines. Their cryptid search turns up a strange nesting site and a pungent scent that is said to be associated with the creature. A piece of evidence leads to a lengthy and memorable pursuit as they contend with dangerous collapsed bridges and deadly snakes. Will these dangers affect their hunt for this Filipino mystery primate?

Josh: "Okay everybody, welcome to Fiji!" **Group**: "Yay!" **Josh**: "We're going to a cannibal village." **Group**: "Boo!"

Josh VO: "I was also puzzled by the variety of unusual looking souvenirs." **Josh**: "What is this?" **Vendor**: "Cannibal fork." **Josh**: "A cannibal fork?

What would somebody eat with this?" **Vendor**: "Brains. A man's brain."
Josh: "Ma'am, I don't eat enough brains that I think I need this in my life."

Josh: "*Stargate*? There's a Syfy-themed strip club in this town?"

Season 5, Episode 4
Destinations: Kazakhstan & Sweden
Cases: UFOs & Swedish Lake Monster
Original Air Date: July 24th, 2012

The team takes to uncharted territory with their maiden voyage to Kazakhstan and a rare investigation into UFO lore. In the south-eastern portion of the country, locals have reported strange lights and sightings of humanoid creatures scouring through a local forest. Allegedly, these are the inhabitants of a crashed craft, scavenging for repair materials and constructing a base in the isolated woodland.

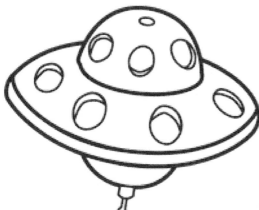

The team is granted access to an odd spherical object recovered from the forest. They embark into the local forest to scour the skies and ground surface for any extraterrestrial activity. In a frightening moment, investigator Kyle Wheeler goes missing after an electrical malfunction while the remaining team members are mesmerized by a sky sighting. Will they uncover both their missing comrade and the identity of the the unusual activity?

Quick, say the name of this aquatic beastie five times fast - Storsjöodjuret! This well publicized creature makes it's home in Lake Storsjön in north-central Sweden, and is the focus of the episode's second half. "The Great Lake Serpent" is present on the region's famous archaeological artifact, the Frösö Rune Stone, which is a relic leftover from the 11th Century. Many expeditions have been launched to locate and even ensnare the beast, but to no avail so far. Team Truth is seeking to remedy that.

They begin their hunt with a daytime aerial sweep and deploy the ROV camera. Their night time expedition takes them into freezing temperatures, seeking the origin of fascinating witness videos. Unusual evidence leads the team one step closer to deciphering this Scandinavian enigma.

Josh: "Nothing like that warm and fuzzy Soviet architecture. Just as many guns as you can put in there, pretty much. We're as close to the Klingon home world as you're gonna get."

Josh VO: "The mountain peak isn't just renowned for UFO sightings - it's also famous for its local amusement park. Tristant tried to muscle up against the strongest member of our team. That being Ryder." **Ryder**: "They used to call me Thor on the Rugby team…oh my God! Did you just hit yourself in the face?!" **Tristant**: "That thing has quite a recoil on it."

Josh VO: "Ryder opted for a burger." **Vendor**: "It's made of moose meat." **Ryder**: "Oh yeah, Bullwinkle tastes delicious."

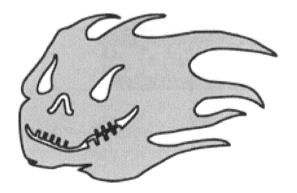

Season 5, Episode 5
Destinations: Guatemala & Fiji
Cases: Tikal Spirits & Lagoon Creature
Original Air Date: July 31st, 2012

Tikal was a major city at the height of Mayan rule in Guatemala. At its peak, the city hosted near 80,000 citizens. It remained a major facet of Meso-American culture through the Classic Period, dating to around the 10th Century. It was around that time period that the city began to decline and ultimately collapsed like the rest of the dynamic culture.

The site of Tikal's massive amount of temples and pyramids are said to play host to spirits from the height of the Mayan empire. The *DT* crew's harrowing trek into the jungle ruins are set upon by several frightening wildlife confrontations. Equipment malfunctions and mysterious lights only further plague the expedition. These ruins have immense history and with the violent acts that blight its past, one must wonder what spiritual energy the site will yield.

Information is rather scarce on this aquatic apex predator that we hear of in the episode's second half. It is your classic sea-faring beast, save that it trades the usual serpentine shape for a stockier, and more powerful barrel shaped body. Think along the lines of the Mosasaurus from *Jurassic World*, yet not nearly as large or opportunistic!

In a slight twist, this un-named creature is said to inhabit the local mangrove swamps as opposed to stalking a local lake or the open ocean. The beast has been stalking Fiji, and the team travels to the village of Savusavu for their latest night time aquatic hunt. What evidence will Josh, Ryder and the crew acquire in the swamps with their trusty ROV camera?

Josh VO: "We breezed through customs in Belize City, hopped into our 4X4, and immediately noticed a national obsession with driver awareness."
Josh: "Okay everybody, keep an eye out for snakes. Watch out guys, turkeys. Keep an eye out for whatever that thing is. And jaguars. That's the only one that really deserves a sign, I think."

Josh: "This is like the baggage belt to nowhere. That is Amelia Earhart's suitcase. That has been on there for 75 years."

Season 5, Episode 6
Destinations: Romania & Sweden
Cases: Vampires & Island Spirits
Original Air Date: August 7th, 2012

Surprisingly it's taken until now, the penultimate episode of the entire series, for an investigation to involve that classic staple of horrific lore - the vampire. One of the most enduring supernatural legends in human history just might be based on a true life cryptozoological marvel. The venue is a forest outside of Sighișoara, childhood home to Vlad Tepes AKA Vlad the Impaler. Although the notorious sadist himself was not a blood drinking supernatural beast, his legacy inspired one of the most classic villains in horror fiction and has darkened the surrounding region.

Team Truth delves into the dark forest, seeking an answer for a rash of livestock mutilations. Their search intensifies as they find the skeletal remains of various animals. The *Blair Witch* itself would feel pangs of homesickness for the abandoned building that the team locates in the wilderness. What horrors lie within, and how do they link with the age old legend of the *Nosferatu*?

In the Baltic sea off the southern coast of Sweden lies a small island known as Blå Jungfrun. This speck of land is notorious for its most distinguishing feature, being a series of stones arranged in a maze-like spiral known as "the labyrinth". This odd feature is known to be cursed and the island itself holds massive magical energy. It is said to be a haven for witches who gather there on Maundy Thursday, which is the Thursday before Easter, which I kid you not, is when this very case description is being written for this book. You can't even plan stuff like that!

Josh and team embark to the island, eager to scan the small forest, its lone cabin and the labyrinth stone feature. With but a small area to search and no inhabitants on the island, the chance for outside interference is slim to nil. Tales also tell of spirits, both benevolent and evil, making their home on the enchanted land and the team encounters plenty of odd happenings as they peruse the cabin and the rock maze. What will happen when the crew reaches the center of the maze, and what spirits allegedly haunt this mystical, mysterious land?

Josh VO: "When it comes to creature popularity contests, there's no question that the Homecoming King of Monsters is the Vampire. From *Twilight* to *True Blood* to the Olsen twins, these pale insomniacs are Kings of pop culture."

Ryder: "I was just having this terrible dream that we were on this awful, awful long train ride." **Josh**: "It's happening, Ryder."

Local Psychic: "I think you're going to have a better designation in your career-" **Josh**: "Better than hosting *DT*? Not possible, ma'am! I'm at the pinnacle of my career right now." **Psychic**: "You are?" **Josh**: "No, I'm not."

Season 5, Episode 7
Destinations: Philippines & Kazakhstan

There is an interesting and fascinating burial custom that takes place in other parts of the world: hanging coffins. Here, they honor the dead by stacking caskets high up and hanging from mountainsides and cliff faces. This in turn keeps the interred safe from scavenging insects and rodents.

One of the most famous sites of hanging coffins is located in the Mountain Province of Sagada in the Phillipines. This fascinating site is also said to be the local haunt for various restless spirits, hovering about their earthly, aerial resting grounds.

The team sets off for the Echo Valley portion of the rural province, but not before Josh and Ryder make a hilarious recreation of the pottery scene from *Ghost*, then making their perilous journey towards the burial site.

 SAD FACT

The Season 5 mid-season finale, which ended up being the series finale, was on Ryder's birthday.
At least we still have Ryder!

The Tian Shan mountains are a majestic range that borders China, Kazakhstan and Uzbekistan. It may also be home to the Kiyik Adam (pronounced "Kee-yook Uh-Dom"), a massive and aggressive hairy hominoid. Of note of this particular beast is its alleged ferocity and massive height. Soaring near ten feet tall, this beast may be the largest of all our primates.

It all comes down to this; the final televised investigation. After years of exciting paranormal and cryptid investigations coupled with thrilling adventure, it all comes to a close. What more can we say? On with the recap!

The *DT* crew travels to Kazakhstan and performs their most unique aerial recon. They employ a falconer to send his bird on a scouting flight! They encounter odd whistling sounds that they amplify with the parabolic dish and find themselves pursuing something into the Kazakhstan night. Will the team manage to track down their latest hairy giant quarry? Is the presence of a lunar eclipse symbolic towards the future of *Destination Truth*?

Richie: "I'm doing good - how you doin'?" **Josh**: "Hanging off a wall is bad enough. Doing it next to 25 coffins is pretty terrifying…world's scariest EVP session starting now."

Josh: "Alright everybody, welcome to Kazakhstan. Ryder, what is the number one rule?" **Ryder**: "No *Borat* jokes." **Josh**: "That is correct. That movie did not go over well here." **Ryder**: "I LIKE!" **Josh**: "Easy."

SEASON FIVE MILESTONES:

- **S5 E1 -** The first time we were given a formal welcoming back to the audience to a new season from host Josh Gates via voice over
- **S5 E2 -** Popular fan request to revisit Hoia Bochu Forest granted and Evan B. Stone returns for this investigation after not being on the show since Season Three
- **S5 E7 -** The unexpected final episode of *DT*

ACKNOWLEDGEMENTS

Other than the credited fan art in the book, additional photography is from Melissa Tapley, Brad Acevedo, Justin Wanamaker, Barbara Perry, behind the scenes from Ping Pong Productions, Kim Knox, and Kat Sanzo. The magnets in the Josh chapter collage are made by Lisa Gage.

I apologize for anyone I forgot in any of the Chapters or in these Acknowledgements - everyone who was part of *DT*'s success, from those who made the show to those who helped promote it on social media, deserves a pat on the back for what they did, and you have my gratitude.

First, a few big thank you's. Thank YOU, to the fellow fan, who took the time to buy and read this book. You have no idea how much it meant to me and my co-author, Brad. I hope you feel my gratitude radiating off the pages.

Obviously, I have to thank Joshua Gates. You've been a mentor and you always looked out for me, despite the fact that for a long time, I was just some fan. Without doing fan promotion and interviews with you, going to the conventions you went to, etcetera, my life wouldn't be what it is. But I've kissed your butt enough, haha so moving on!

Thanks to Hallie and to Josh's parents, who have always been nice to me when I've seen them at events. To Owen, when you're old enough to read this - you have some cool parents. Don't be one of those jaded kids who thinks their parents are lame and be sure to take up the lessons your dad has spread to many people - how important travel is, how vital it is to understand other cultures, and to keep an open mind. Your mom has also helped a lot of people, so never be afraid to go to her for anything.

To my family and my friends - thanks for the help, through car rides or what have you, and interest in me doing this fan work. Dad and Pam are the rockstars on that list. To Brad - it's such a treat to find someone so similar to myself. Someone who encourages my crazy ideas, including this book, but someone to also get me to calm down or laugh, when I needed it. Thank you for being YOU. The secret word is LOVE - AHHHHHH!

Thanks to Aislynn, Michelle, Erika and Mendy for helping with the fan page social media and other tasks, as well as helping to promote *Stranded* for it's one season of airing. You're great friends, as well.

Thanks to Christiane and her husband for helping me with the fan site and helping me get to my first SDCC convention in 2010, including additional thanks to Christiane for having a camera with a good battery on it, so we could get that Colin Ferguson interview on video!

To some people who I doubt will ever see this - Thanks to Marc Tetlow at Ideal Event Management. Thanks to Maureen at Syfy who was able to get me into the Syfy Press Event in 2009, as well as other fun and awesome events that Josh was apart of. You really helped build this fan community, without ever knowing it. Also, thanks to Gary and Craig at Syfy, as well. Despite the gripes fans had, and have, with Syfy, they have really decent people who worked there who were just doing just that - their jobs.

Also, thanks to Morgan Spurlock, who interviewed me about my fan promo work for *DT* and for putting me, even for a second, in one of his documentaries. True bucket list item! Thanks to Kenn, Wes and Sophia for being the first people who interviewed me about this book, while we're on the topic of journalism.

Thanks to Ping Pong Productions, especially Brad, for including me and this fan site in on projects on an intimate level where I could be excited and share that excitement with fans. Some places will just send you a press kit, or in my case, a PDF press release, since it costs less to ship. Ping Pong's hands on approach with their viewers, however, and with the press, makes all the difference. I also, on the same level, want to thank Neil Mandt and Matt Nix for sharing with me materials from Josh's earlier projects.

I want to give a special thanks to Donald James, who did the show voice overs of *DT* for NBC Universal Asia. We did a great interview on how to get into voice over work, and he also recorded a super fun intro for *DT Fan Radio* that was used for most of the episodes. Thanks, Donald!

Here is a list of *DT* cast members I interviewed on *DT Fan Radio*, who I thank for their time with not only me, but my fellow fans. Here are the dates the cast was interviewed or their recorded interviews aired on *DT Fan Radio* (you can find these on iTunes via the Podcast category for looking for the terms "DT fan radio" or "mandogg house radio":

- Josh Gates - 7/12/2009, 9/4/2009, 10/9/2009, 3/24/2010, 9/9/2010, 10/6/2010, 3/11/2011, 9/27/2011, 10/7/2011, 7/12/2011, 7/31/2012, 2/20/2013, 1/26/2015
- Erin Ryder - 10/6/2010, 3/11/2011, 12/1/2011, 7/12/2012
- Brad Kuhlman - 10/9/2009, 3/24/2010, 3/11/2011
- Rex Williams - 9/15/2009, 6/12/2010,
- Jael de Pardo - 10/22/2009, 5/19/2010, 10/29/2010
- Ramy Romany - 2/14/2011
- Troy Tackett - 7/19/2009
- Shawn Goodwin - 9/16/2010
- Gabe Copeland - 9/15/2009
- Casey Brumels - 12/1/2011

List of *DT* cast members, in no particular order:
- Joshua Gates (Seasons 1 through 5)
- Erin Ryder (Seasons 2, 3, 4 & 5)
- Gabriel Copeland (Seasons 3 & 4)
- Rex Williams (Seasons 3 & 4)

- Jael de Pardo (Seasons 3 & 4)
- Evan Stone (Seasons 3 & 5)
- Sharra Jenkins-Romany (Season 3)
- Casey Brumels (Season 2)
- Jarrod Tomassi (Season 2)
- Ali Zubik (Season 4)
- Jed Udall (Season 2)
- Mike Morrell (Seasons 3 & 4)
- Tony Gonzales (Season 4)
- Shawn Goodwin (Season 4)
- Chris Lore (Season 4)
- Allie Boettger (Season 4)
- Kyle Wheeler (Seasons 4 & 5)
- David D'Angelo (Season 5)
- Katy Maurakami (Season 5)
- Adam Butler (Season 5)
- Tristant Icaza (Season 5)
- Richie Fung (Season 5)
- Eric Wing (Season 1)
- Lindsay Gillette (Season 1)
- Erica "Shush" Shusha (Season 2)
- Marc Carter (Season 1)
- Aracelli Haldeman (Season 2)
- Vanessa Joy Smith (Season 4)
- Dan Ramirez (Season 4)
- Terry Brown AKA "T-Bone" (Season 2)
- Hank Braxtan (Season 1)
- Michael St. Hilaire AKA "Ponch" (Season 1)
- Bechara "Bicha" Golum (Season 3)
- Bobby Pura (Season 4)
- Producers who appeared on the show - Neil Mandt (Season 1) & Brad Kuhlman (Season 2)
- Special mention to Jeff Rice (RIP)

References to Interviews Conducted or Resources used for this book:
- *DT Fan Radio* episodes mentioned
- Credit to Syfy, Mandt Brothers Productions and Ping Pong Productions for *DT* quotes and show intros referenced

- iTunes was used as a reference for first air dates for *DT*, *Stranded* and *Insane or Inspired*?
- *Stranded* cancellation notice: http://renewcanceltv.com/stranded-cancelled-season-2/
- Josh's *DT* cancelation announcement, dated March 27th of 2014 http://www.twitlonger.com/show/n_1s15nsi
- Josh Gates acting credits http://www.imdb.com/name/nm1239433/
- About *Destination Dinners* http://www.paranormalpopculture.com/2012/04/josh-gates-destination-dinner-to-serve.html
- King Tut story reference: http://www.cnn.com/2016/01/24/africa/king-tut-broken-mask-charges/
- Special thanks to those who made destinationtruth.wikia.com and Josh's *Wikipedia* pages for some extra info
- SingularityFanPages.com archive for other references
- Saul Rubinek interview in the *Warehouse 13* press room at SDCC 2011, documented on YouTube
- Josh interview in the *Sanctuary* press room at SDCC 2011 - documented on YouTube
- *Sanctuary* panel Q&A at SDCC 2011 - documented on YouTube
- Multiple interviews at the *Eureka* press room at SDCC 2010 - documented on YouTube
- Multiple interviews at the *Warehouse 13* press room at SDCC 2010 - documented on YouTube
- Dustin Pari YouTube interview at "A Night with Attleboro Paranormal" at the Attleboro Public Library in MA in December of 2011
- October 15th 2011 YouTube interview with Amy and Adam of *Ghost Hunters*
- February 6th 2012 interview with Nick Groff on BlogTalkRadio and documented on YouTube

LIST OF JOSH GATES' MAJOR PROJECTS:
- *Beg, Borrow & Deal* - reality show contestant, 2002
- BMW Commercial - actor, 2002
- Short Films Acted In: *Singularity, Carpet Diem, Cookie de Mayo, Hard Cell* & *Party Foul* (all short films were pre-*Destination Truth*)
- *Flavor of Love* - reality show, waiter/actor, 2006

- Narrated the audio book for *A Brother's Journey* by Richard B. Pelzer in 2008 - this won him the Earphones Award from *Audiofile Magazine*
- Budweiser's *Truly Famous* mini series* - actor
- *Destination Truth* - host & producer, 2007 to 2012
- *Ghost Hunters Live* - multiple years of hosting gigs
- *Ghost Hunters* - multiple years of guest investigator cameos
- *Ghost Hunters Int'l* - cameo, 2008
- *Destination Truth Live* - host & investigator, 2011
- Josh's Book *Memoirs of a Monster Hunter* released 2011
- Hosted day-long Saturday St. Patty's Day Syfy Movie Marathon, 2012
- *Insane or Inspired* - celebrity on-screen commentary, 2012
- *Fact or Faked* - guest investigator, 2012
- *Stranded* - produced & narrated, 2013
- *Doggy Nightmares* - narrated, 2013
- *Hacking the System* - produced, 2014
- *Expedition Unknown* - host & producer, 2015 to present
- *The Trip* - celebrity on-screen guest, 2016

*Unsure of the release year for this project. Available for the public to view on YouTube.

Significant Josh Gates interviews - Larry King, the Today Show, Good Morning America, KTLA, the Hallmark Channel & CNN (plus many more)

BONUS!

If you made it to the end of this book, here are some fun Easter Eggs, for you. Because it's sad you are done reading this book, as sad as it is that I'm done writing it, let's leave you off with three funny quotes.

"(Reading off of a t-shirt in poorly written English) "'New Dimensfons of Wide Variations from graceful images to ethnic tones resppeared colorfully. Everlasting & prolound taste being able to be reproduced by natural materials.' That is the CRAZIEST shirt I've ever seen in my life!" -**Josh, from a *Syfy.com* bonus scene in a Japanese department store**

Josh: "Mike, I'm dying. I'm gonna need to pass the torch to the next generation of monster hunter. This is it for me." Mike: "It's too soon, it's too soon." Josh: "I've had a good run! (pretending to cry) I've had a good run, Mike!" Rex: "My advice would be just giving it an injection. Just one injection, get it out of the way. Takes up less time. Same reaction you get from it, same benefit." Josh: "Where does the injection go?" Rex: "It goes into your butt." Josh: "God, it's never easy, or pleasant. God, why can't it ever just be easy?!" -**From a *Syfy.com* bonus scene, where Josh has a fast-moving infection in his leg in a Romanian forrest**

"I have a very troubled relationship *with Guitar Hero*." -**Josh, March 23rd 2010 DT Fan Radio episode**

Made in the USA
Coppell, TX
09 December 2019